# WORD HUNTERS

## THE LOST HUNTERS

# NICK EARLS &
# TERRY WHIDBORNE

UQP

First published 2013 by University of Queensland Press
PO Box 6042, St Lucia, Queensland 4067 Australia
Reprinted 2015

www.uqp.com.au
uqp@uqp.uq.edu.au

Typeset in 11/16pt Horley Old Style by Jo Hunt
Printed in Australia by McPherson's Printing Group

**Cataloguing-in-Publication Data**
*National Library of Australia*

Earls, Nick, 1963-
The lost hunters / Nick Earls and Terry Whidborne.

Earls, Nick, 1963- Word hunters ; 2.

For primary school age.

Whidborne, Terry.

ISBN (pbk) 978 0 7022 4958 7
ISBN (pdf) 978 0 7022 5072 9
ISBN (epub) 978 0 7022 5073 6
ISBN (kindle) 978 0 7022 5074 3

A823.3

University of Queensland Press uses papers that are natural, renewable and recyclable products made from wood grown in sustainable forests. The logging and manufacturing processes conform to the environmental regulations of the country of origin.

While stories build from words, it's true,

The words themselves have stories too.

Who dares to read? Who dares to look?

Who dares to hunt within this book?

$\mathcal{T}$HE LAST PHOTO of Alan Hunter was taken on the day he went missing. He taught Year 5 at Cubberla Creek State School, and it was sports day. In the photo he wore an orange towelling hat, shorts that were pulled up way too high and socks that went to just below his knees. He had a megaphone in his hand and a vinyl bag over one shoulder with 'TAA' and a picture of a plane on it. In other words, according to Lexi and Al's father close to 30 years later, he looked like a classic daggy teacher from 1983.

Even in that photo, Lexi now thought she could see a key pinned to her grandfather's shirt – a key exactly like the ones she and Al had used to lock their word hunters' pegs in place.

It was Lexi's turn to dust the lounge room, a job that always took ages because of the number of framed photos on the bookshelves. Al was on the back deck cleaning the barbecue. He complained every time that it was the worse job of the two, but he never wanted to swap.

Lexi took the photo into the kitchen, where their father was tying a bin bag.

'Do you know what that is?' She pointed to the key in the photo. 'I've always wondered.'

Al's face appeared at the window, glaring at her. He couldn't believe she'd brought it up and drawn attention to it.

Their father took the photo, then stretched his arm out and squinted at it. 'No. I'll need some help.' His reading glasses were at the end of the bench, and he put them on. 'Oh, that. It's a badge Grandad Al wore. He had it for a couple of years. He wore it a lot. I always assumed it was a Lions Club badge, or Rotary, or something.'

'I didn't know he was in any of those,' Al said through the screen. He had his hands next to his face to shield himself from the glare outside.

'Well, I don't know that he was.' Their father took another look at the photo. 'I don't remember him going to any meetings. I just think that's what it was. I never asked him about it.' He handed the photo back to Lexi. 'I was 15. If it had been Rotary and I'd sounded interested, he would have had me on the school Interact club executive the next day. That's like junior Rotary. Or it was, back then.' He waved his hand in front of his face at the smell of the rubbish in the bin bag. 'I've got to get this out of the house.'

He finished tying it and picked up the plastic recycling bin, which was full of bottles and crushed cereal boxes.

Al stayed at the window. As soon as their father was gone he said, 'What were you thinking? You could blow the whole thing.'

'Well, I didn't. And I wouldn't. Not with that.' Lexi put the photo down on the bench. 'We've got to find out what we can. Grandad Al is lost somewhere in the – I don't know – last few thousand years? Thirty years ago he chased a word into the past and it went wrong. The only people who know that, and the only people who have any chance of finding him, are you and me. And if I can find one clue in the present that'll get us to him sooner and save me from having to fight the Battle of Hastings again – or any other stupid war – I'll take it.'

The front screen door squeaked and slapped shut. Their father was back from the bins.

'Okay,' Al said before he came in. 'But there's got to be a better way.'

'A family history project.' Mursili was pacing up and down in his office in the school library when the idea came to him. 'I'll find some way of making it official. Or making it look official.' He picked up a sheet of school letterhead and fed it into his printer. 'I know – something about confidentiality. About how family details won't be disclosed, et cetera, et cetera. Get your parents to sign it, saying they understand the terms. That's very 21st century.' He smiled and nodded. 'Imagine if I'd suggested that to King Suppi back in Hattusa. Getting peasants to sign something, as if they had some say. Hah. Far too dangerous. Where would it end?'

Al swivelled around in one of the chairs next to Mursili's desk. 'Dad's an architect and Mum's an accountant.'

Mursili wasn't listening. He was pushing buttons on the printer. Al was sure they'd had architects and accountants in Hattusa, even if it had been more than three thousand years ago. The palace hadn't built itself, and part of Mursili's job had been looking after the financial records. Al still wasn't clear on everything Mursili had done, but he'd been left in no doubt about how important it was.

'You have King Suppi,' Mursili had told him one day, marking the air with his hand, head high. 'Then you have the generals and the ministers and the high priests of the temples. And of course the court librarian.' Neck high. 'Below that, everyone is just following orders, making baskets, threshing grain, standing watch in the towers.' Both his hands had then waved around imprecisely somewhere lower down, as if those people hadn't mattered much.

'But what if someone worked out the letter was a fake?' Lexi said as Al did another couple of spins in his chair and Mursili sat down at his desk. 'Couldn't you get in trouble? Couldn't we all get in trouble?'

Mursili shrugged. 'What can they do? Transfer me back to my old job? I don't think so. Take my liver to the mountain and feed it to gryphons? You don't do that here.' He started typing. 'Anyway, we get your parents to sign things all the time. Working bee? Sign here. Understand the new

5

contagious diseases policy? Sign here.' He was concentrating hard, typing with two fingers, but trying to make himself use at least four. 'Sacrifice a few goats to appease the rain gods? Sign here.'

Lexi cleared her throat. 'I think that one's from the old days.'

Mursili wasn't listening. 'Home keys, home keys,' he reminded himself. He had a touch-typing manual open on his desk. He hit 'print' and pushed his chair back from the keyboard. 'I hope you find him soon. Your grandfather. I hope the family history project gives you something that helps, or at least confirms what you're thinking. The dictionary hasn't—' He tried to think of the right way to put it. 'Signalled you? Sent you anywhere?'

'Not for two weeks,' Al said. 'Nearly two weeks. We'll call you as soon as it does anything.'

'Good.' Mursili picked the letter up from the printer, checked it and folded it. 'We need to get you as ready as we can. Information's the key, I think. Forewarned is forearmed, as they say.' He reached for an envelope. 'Though much use it was when the Kaskians burnt our fields on the way to Hattusa.'

The silver recorder sat on the coffee table with its red light on as Grandma Noela confirmed that Grandad Al hadn't been a member of a Lions or Rotary club.

'I thought the badge was something to do with school,' she said. She had her own set of photos, far more of them than

their father. 'I thought it was a craft club. I might have even asked him once, and I think he told me that. Or debating. Yes, something to do with words.' She looked again at the photo in her hand. Grandad Al was on a jetty, holding up a fish he had caught. He was wearing the orange towelling hat again. He had a peg key pinned to his collar. 'He did lots of things for the kids, lots of extra things. They loved him, you know.'

Grandma Noela had made fruitcake, and she cut Al a third piece without even thinking. She had photo albums full of family pictures, but Grandad Al had taken most of them and only appeared here and there. He was the same height as Lexi and Al's father, and had similar hair. Their father's hair was starting to recede. He was two years older than Grandad Al had been when he disappeared.

In the last two years of photos, though, Grandad Al had changed – not a lot, but it was there if you looked for it. On

7

his wedding day he had been a thin man with slick black hair and a dark suit, and over the years he had put on weight. Over the last two years, though, he had lost it. He looked stronger. The muscles in his arms were more defined.

'He looks very healthy,' Al said, to see how Grandma Noela might react.

'Oh, yes.' She put the fishing photo down next to one from a few years before. It only made the contrast clearer. 'He decided to look after himself. He was pretty determined about it too. His father had had heart trouble. I think that's what did it. He and your dad started doing a lot of bushwalking. Sometimes they'd go out for days with practically nothing – just some food and a compass. Sometimes your grandfather would go by himself. Survival training, he called it. And he learnt to ride a horse. He said he'd wanted to since he was very young, but his family could never afford it. And he went to fencing classes – you know, fighting with swords. He said it was good for balance and coordination.'

Al stopped chewing in the middle of a mouthful. He knew what it meant. He could tell Lexi did too. In the early 1980s Grandad Al, without telling anyone, had turned himself into a medieval warrior.

'I have something more,' Grandma Noela said. 'It's probably the time for you to see it, if you're working on a family history project.'

She stood up and went down the hall to her bedroom. They could hear her opening a cupboard.

8

'Do you think that's what we've got to do?' Lexi turned the two photos on the table around to get a better look at them. 'Learn how to ride horses and fight with swords?'

'We want to find him,' Al said. 'So, yeah. Maybe it is what we have to do.'

Lexi had wanted the answer to be no. She had wanted Al to have another way. The wounds on her arm from the Battle of Hastings had only just healed, but the scars were still pink.

'You should probably cut down on the cake then,' she told him. 'People don't get themselves ready for battle by hoovering up cake.'

'Because you'd know.' He shoved another piece in his mouth.

'Hey, I already fought two battles and the food was terrible both times. No cake.'

Grandma Noela came out of her room with a box in her hands. She sat down between them again, put her glasses on and opened it. She lifted out a folder of yellowing newspaper clippings.

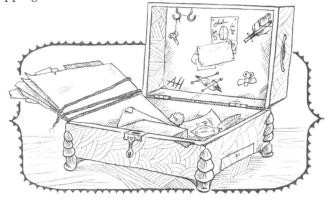

9

'One of my friends cut these out,' she said. 'She gave them to me later, in case I ever wanted to have them. The other things in there are from your grandad's desk at school. The police kept them for a while.'

She took her glasses off and rubbed her eyes. The clippings were all about Grandad Al's disappearance.

'If you're writing family histories at Cubberla Creek, this is a story you can't avoid.' She sat back in her seat. She didn't want to look. 'I'm going to make myself another cup of tea, I think. You can ask me any questions you need to, though.'

She stood up again, and Al moved his knees so that she could walk past.

'I want to help her,' Lexi said once Grandma was in the kitchen. 'I've never seen her feeling this bad.'

'We *can* help her. And no one else can.' Al leant forward and picked up an article. 'There's one way.' They had to go back into the past, as many times as it took to find Grandad Al. 'I hope he's okay. I hope he's just stuck.'

The newspapers had started out with big stories about his disappearance. It made several front pages. They ran the sports day photo and talked about what a popular teacher he was and how out of character it was for him to disappear. They mentioned his bushwalking, but also said that his habit was to plan each walk well in advance and to make sure Grandma Noela knew exactly where he was going and when he'd be back. There was no plan this time: it was the middle of a school day and all his bushwalking gear was where it usually was, under the house.

When he stayed missing the papers wrote about him having no known enemies and about there being no leads among his past students. His bank accounts weren't touched. He contacted no one. He was never seen. There was a picture of police divers searching the creek.

He was gone, with everything he was carrying in the sports day photo. There was simply no trace.

One article talked about his 'health kick' of the past couple of years, and his interest in survival skills. Pictures of him were posted at national parks, but there were no sightings.

A friend mentioned that he'd had quite a few unexplained injuries over the years, but she had put them all down to the new activities in his life.

'Hastings,' Lexi said, 'or whatever battles he ended up at.'

'And he kept the dictionary at school, behind the loose panel in the library wall.' It made sense to Al now. 'He checked it on his way to sports day, and it had gone off. A word in it had activated, so he touched it, opened the portal and went after it. He went into the past and got lost, and the dictionary stayed there for 30 years, until they renovated the library.'

In the kitchen, the kettle boiled. They could hear Grandma Noela opening the Tupperware box she kept tea bags in.

'Well, now we get to find him,' Lexi said. 'One day, when the right word comes along.' She leant forward to look into the box. There were pens in there, and paper clips. And an old ship with a pencil sharpener in its stern. She felt sick. 'What if he's the guy we saw in Nantucket? What if we did it? What if we left him there?'

Al looked up fencing lessons online, but the pictures didn't look much like the sword fighting he had seen – or done – in battles in the past.

'We're going to have to learn somehow,' Lexi said when he showed her. 'But you're right. I don't think it'd help us to stand like that.' The caption on the screen said 'lunge' but the move in the picture looked more like poking someone with a wire while sticking your back leg out.

They took peg keys and made them into badges. Lexi had been given a machine that made badges on their tenth birthday, so no one would be surprised by that. Al had even made a few himself. He had one that said 'May contain traces of peanut' and another that said 'If you cannot see my mirrors I cannot see you'.

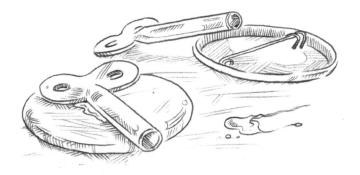

Their father noticed them first. Lexi told him they were doing it for Grandad Al, and that they'd got the idea during the family history project.

'That's a nice thing to do,' he said as he turned the badge over in his hand. 'It even looks like the same kind of key.' He found his glasses and took a closer look at it. 'What do you think it's from? Did this one come with something, or was it just a key?'

'Just a key.' She and Al had planned the answer. 'It's from the craft shop at Indooroopilly. Next to the old buttons.'

'I wonder how your grandfather got them. I can't imagine him in a craft shop.' He took his glasses off. 'Do you think it means something? He wore badges like this quite a bit. I think I just got used to it. I should have asked him.' He shook his head. 'No good thinking that way. We had months of treating practically everything as a clue and it all turned out not to be. You can drive yourself mad doing that. All that survival skills stuff, for instance. I once said to the police that it wouldn't have surprised me if he'd been building a nuclear fallout shelter in the backyard and stocking it with baked beans. It was a joke. The next day your grandma opened the door to a forensics team who'd been sent to check out the shelter.'

Lexi and Al kept their badges on when they could and carried them in pockets when they couldn't. From the photos they had seen, that was what Grandad Al had done. It had meant he was always ready to find a lost hunter, in his own time or any time he landed in the past.

'How many words do you think go through Nantucket in the 1830s?' Lexi was pinning her badge back on as they walked out of school.

'Practically none.' Al hadn't wanted to admit that. 'But some'll go through America, and we can get to Nantucket, if we have time. And he's been gone from here for 30 years, so maybe that means he's been wherever he is for 30 years. If it was him in Nantucket, that puts him in America until the 1860s. Americans come up with lots of words. We'll get there.'

'Okay,' she said, because she didn't want to point out that he was guessing, and they didn't have a clue. 'Okay.'

**Okay:**
adjective, adverb, noun, verb (used with object), interjection.

Agreed, accepted, acceptable, acceptance (to give the okay), to approve. Variant of OK.

& MORE

'Y OU AND I have to go somewhere,' Al said when he found Lexi in the kitchen.

She was standing with the fridge door open. It started to beep at her. 'It's gone off?'

'Just now. It's a good word. It's the kind of word that might help us. I bet it's an American word.'

He could see their parents out on the back deck. Their father was turning sausages on the barbecue and their mother was holding a glass of wine and talking. She was indicating something she wanted to do with the garden, but their father was only half-listening. Al wondered if he had time to eat a couple of sausages. But only briefly.

'It's "okay",' he said.

'How do you know that?' Lexi shut the fridge door.

'It's "okay". The word.'

'Yeah, but how do you *know* it's okay? We practically got massacred every time when the word was "water" and water should have been okay.'

'No, it's—' Al felt like he was on the brink of a comedy routine from one of those old black-and-white TV shows that sometimes ran on the extra digital channels. Their father insisted they'd been funny once. 'Just come.'

Lexi followed him down the hall to his room. The

dictionary was open on his desk. Even with the light on, she could see the blinking gold button from the doorway.

'Oh, "okay",' she said when she looked at it more closely. 'Now I get it.'

'Are we doing this?'

'We're doing it. We agreed.' She stared at the book. It might send them anywhere. It was full of invasion and war and trade and chance, and 'okay' could contain any combination of those. 'Grandad Al's got to be somewhere. I'll shut the door, you call Mursili.'

Al flicked to Mursili's number on his phone and sat down at the desk while he waited for it to be answered. He could feel his heart racing, beating right up in his throat already. He tried to focus on the plan. His bag was packed, and Mursili could give them some idea of what lay ahead. He opened his laptop, got online and started looking for 'okay'.

'Ahoy,' Mursili said, when he answered. 'Do we have something?'

'Yes, we do.' Al switched him to speaker and set the phone down. 'The word is "okay". "O-K-A-Y." I'm going to Wikipedia.'

'All right. I'll do the etymology dictionaries and then go wider.'

Al heard Mursili's phone clunk down onto a hard surface.

'Choctaw,' Lexi said, reading the Wikipedia entry over Al's shoulder. 'It looks like a Native American language. Or West African, from slaves. I really don't want to end up on some slave ship that's grabbing people in Africa hundreds of years ago.'

'No "okay" in this dictionary.' It was Mursili's voice. 'There's "tokay", which is a kind of wine.' They could hear keys clicking. 'All right, found something. I've got someone disputing the Choctaw theory. And the West African, where apparently it's "ki" or "kie", an expression of surprise. Like saying "oh" in English so that sometimes, when they'd learnt English, the slaves said both. "Oh, ki." But that's surprise, not agreement. It's not linked.'

Al scanned the Wikipedia entry. He couldn't concentrate to read it properly. 'Everything else is 19th century American.'

'Yes.' Mursili's mouse clicked next to his phone, and then scraped across his mouse pad. 'Yes, I think that'll be it: 19th century American. Quite a few possibilities there, though. If you can avoid the Civil War, you should be all right.' There was a pause, while Mursili read something more on screen. 'I think that's as close as we can get for now. I'll call you in a minute, to check that you're back safely.' There was another pause. Lexi stared at the phone, wanting to hear something certain and safe, wanting one single good answer about where they were headed. But Mursili just said, 'Good luck,' and that was it.

They were on their own.

Doug was running on his wheel when Al opened the lid of his box. Al reached in and Doug climbed onto his hand, looked up and gave a few quick blinks, which Al took as rat sign language that Doug was ready for the next adventure.

Lexi opened Al's backpack to give it one final check. They'd made a list and she went through it, mentally marking

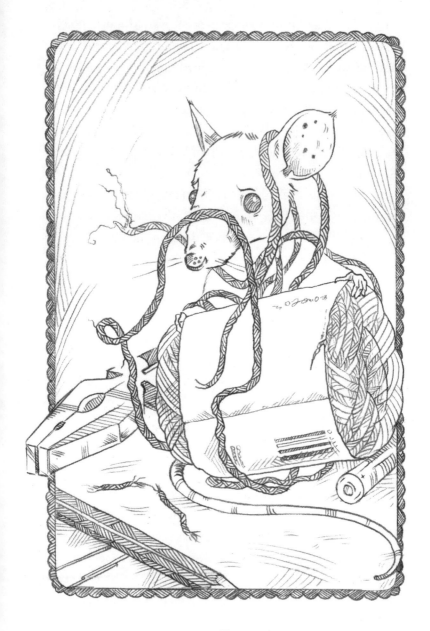

everything off – a knife, two torches, a ball of string, a roll of tape, some pliers in case a peg key broke, the bushwalking first-aid kit …

'First time in my life I've ever looked in a bag and wanted it to have more weapons,' she said.

'This is Fig Tree Pocket.' Al put his arms through the shoulder straps. 'We don't do weapons.'

She went over to the desk and stood in front of the dictionary again. 'Okay?'

'Okay.'

She reached for the '& more' button and pressed it.

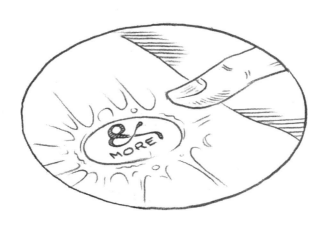

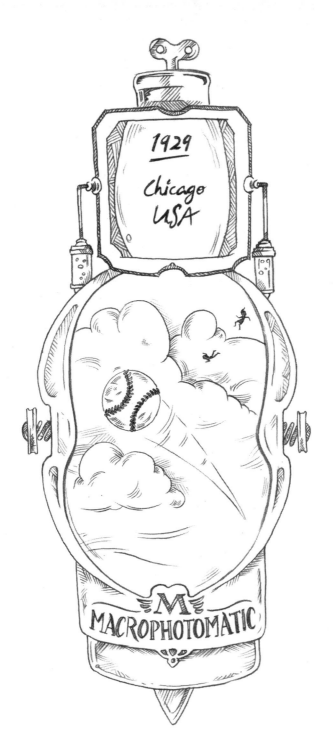

$\mathcal{T}$HE FALL WAS short, with a few small bumps before the cloud opened up. Each bump was a language manual or a book about grammar, and together they felt like moguls on a ski run, with one quick thump immediately followed by the next. From studying his copy of Caractacus's timeline Al knew it went all the way back to 1850, but this run was over almost before it began.

Below them was a lake like a huge grey-blue tongue. They were dropping towards the edge of it, away from the farmlands and forests and towards a city, right to the heart of the city, where it met the water.

They could see baseball diamonds, train lines and a park, but they landed on the flat roof of a building close to ten storeys high.

'Okay,' Lexi said, because it seemed like the right word to use. She checked the roof. They were alone, except for two pigeons on a nearby railing with their heads tucked in against the cold wind blowing from the lake.

There was a sign attached to the front of the building and she could just make out the tops of the letters. It looked as if it was wired to light up at night.

She reached into Al's bag for the peg. 'Chicago, 1929.'

'That's going to mean gangsters,' Al said, as if it might be a good thing.

25

'Of course it is, because they added so much to the language.' Lexi shoved the peg back in the bag. 'I don't want it to be gangsters.'

'But think of who we might meet. Al Capone.'

'Stop. You're not making it better.' She pulled the strap on his bag through the buckle. Somewhere inside, Doug made a muffled noise.

'We're dressed to meet gangsters.' Al wasn't stopping. He had baggy pants with braces, a white shirt and a cap. His key badge was now on his braces. Lexi was in a maid's uniform, with her badge on her collar. 'Maybe I run messages for them. Maybe you – I don't know. Maybe you dust their machine guns. You look like you're in a silent movie.'

'We both do.' Lexi had a lacy kind of hat on her head, and she moved it to make it less uncomfortable. 'It's the 1920s. This is how everyone looks in old movies.'

'How many pegs?'

'I didn't check.' She looked over the edge, at the big black cars on the street and the delivery boys slipping between them on bikes. 'Someone distracted me by talking about gangsters.'

'They only ever got Al Capone for tax evasion.' Al swung the bag from his back. 'We'll be okay.'

He had a foothold on the past again and he was loving it. Chicago, 1929. He couldn't remember who was real and who wasn't – Bugsy Malone or Bugsy Siegel. There were too many movies, but this was the real thing – the place and the time when law-breakers and law-makers fought each other from the running boards of big dark cars.

He unbuckled the bag. Doug climbed out and sniffed the air, but it was too cold to carry much more than the smell of smoke.

In the bag, the tape, the string and almost everything was just as Al had packed it, though now with word pegs on top. He counted five of them. He would definitely have told Lexi if there had been three, and maybe four. She wouldn't want to hear that there were five. But something was missing. He ran through the contents again in his head.

'The knife's gone.' He lifted up a pair of gloves, but there was nothing under them. 'Did you take it out?'

'Of course not. You saw me. You probably—' She was going to say that he had probably forgotten to put it in there, but she had seen it. 'It was there. I don't know what's happened.'

It was another question for Caractacus. Where had the knife gone? *Why* had the knife gone? They would have to make a list of questions and put it in Al's bag too, for the next time they were in the 5th century.

'At least it's America,' Al said, looking across the buildings of the wintry city as smoke spilt from factory chimneys and the noise of traffic came up from the street. 'And we haven't overshot the 1830s yet. If it was Grandad Al back then in Nantucket, he won't be here, but at least we're on our way.'

They checked the roof for anything that might help them, but there was nothing there except pigeon poo and a few broken bottles.

They found an unlocked door that led to stairs and, as Al stepped inside, Lexi said, 'Hey, no initials. Not yet, anyway. No sign that any other word hunters have been here. Do you think we're in the right place? Are we going wrong already?'

'We came straight down. If we'd flown off course, maybe. No, we're where we should be.' He led the way down the stairs. 'It's 1929. Most word hunters come from before then anyway, so they wouldn't have done this step.' Grandad Al would have, though, if he'd done 'okay'. Grandad Al came from more than 50 years later, and wrote 'AH' in blue pen each time. 'Maybe the initials are somewhere in the building.'

He wanted to find the blue 'AH'. He wanted 'okay' to take them right to Grandad Al. Every step along the way there was a new portal to find – a new portal they might *not* find. Grandad Al was a teacher and a veteran word hunter, and he'd missed one somewhere. Al wanted to see initials: any sign they weren't off course.

They stopped at the first floor they came to, at a door with the number 8 on it. When he put his ear to it, Al had a gambling den in mind – gangsters, jazz, the whir of a roulette wheel, bottles of illegal drink clinking on a trolley – but all he could hear were voices and feet on a hard floor. Sometimes maybe the past wasn't interesting – it was just getting on with business.

'We landed on the roof,' Lexi said. 'Not at the front door down on the street. Maybe whatever we've got to do happens high up. I reckon we give it a go.'

Al pushed the door open.

Whatever went on in the building, it was no gambling den and everyone was moving quickly. Men crossed the corridor from one door to another, carrying documents as if they were in a hurry. All around was the sound of typing, hands typing at high speed and pages being pulled from typewriters with a zipping sound.

'Copy!' someone in one of the rooms shouted. 'Copy!' It was clearly a demand.

A boy dressed like Al ducked into the room and left about a second later, separating sheets of paper as he ran.

'I'm one of those,' Al said to Lexi. 'Whatever they are.'

A man stuck his head out of the nearest doorway. 'Copy boy,' he said to Al. He had sheets of paper in his hand. 'This one's not for the subs. It's for the board meeting. Take it there now, would you?'

'You have submarines?' Al said, before he could think it through.

'What? Submarines?' The man stopped checking the pages. Then he worked it out and laughed. 'Oh, you must be new. We have sub-editors, not submarines. They fix up the garbage some of these guys write. But this isn't for them. These are the style guide updates for the year. Every newspaper has a style guide to keep its work consistent. The board needs to sign off on any changes. Last door down the hall.' He pointed into the distance, then held the documents out for Al to take before stepping back into his office.

Al read the top page. 'It's a newspaper. That's what they do here. They're writing for a newspaper.'

On the way down the corridor, they passed other offices where people were typing at desks, and a photographers' darkroom.

'Girl!' someone called out as they got closer to the boardroom.

It was an older woman with small glasses and her hair in a bun. She called Lexi into a room that turned out to be a kitchen and storeroom. Al waited a few steps down the hall, straightening the pages. He tried not to think of the one time they had been separated, when Lexi had been captured in the New Forest in 1100. But this was Chicago in the 20th century, a newspaper office, a time and place he almost understood.

'They have coffee already,' the woman said to Lexi, 'but I want you to make certain they never need to ask for more, and that they have plenty of cigarettes. Take some and refill the boxes on the table now. They may also need more iced water.'

The woman gave her a carton of cigarettes. Lexi had seen people smoking at work in old movies, and now she was supplying some of those people with the cigarettes.

The door to the boardroom was clear enough. It had 'Boardroom' on it in gold letters. Al knocked.

'Come in.' Whoever owned the voice sounded kinder than the woman with the bun or the people shouting, 'Copy!' It turned out to be the man at the head of the table. 'One each, please,' he said when he saw what Al was holding. 'I'm assuming those are the style guide updates?'

'That's right, sir,' Al said.

He worked his way along the table, placing a copy in front of each of the men sitting around it. The smoke in the air made Doug cough and Al coughed to cover it, but no one seemed to notice. The windows in the room were all shut. Lexi took cigarettes from the carton and filled the silver box at one end of the table. A man reached out and took one right away, and lit a match.

'Next up,' the man chairing the meeting said, 'the Academy of Motion Picture Arts and Sciences is intending to make its awards an annual event, and the name "Academy of Motion Picture Arts and Sciences Awards"—' He shrugged. 'Anyone not asleep yet? The name is unbearably long. So we'll be cutting it down to "Academy Awards". Give it a year or two. People will get used to it. Then we've got "big shot".'

'That's gangster talk,' one of the others said. It was the man who had just lit the cigarette. He shook the match and it went out. 'You're going to have the boys writing in gangster talk?'

'It started out as gangster talk.' The chairman glanced down at his notes. 'Regular people say it now. It's not about the calibre of your gun anymore. It's about being in a position of power, or getting big ideas about your own importance. "You think you're such a big shot." You hear people saying that.' He looked around the table, but no one had anything to add. 'I think that's the lot, but I've had Henry put it all in writing for each of your departments.'

He took a copy of the style guide update from Al, and checked the first page before turning it over.

'No, there's one more,' he said. 'Page two. "Okay."'

'How's that work?' one of the other men said. 'I thought it was just an "O" and a "K".'

'It was. But it's become a word. It's generally accepted as one, so we're proposing to spell it as one. We're a newspaper. It's up to us to take the lead.'

The other man stared at the word on the page, weighing it up. 'Well,' he said, 'if that's the case, I guess "O-K-A-Y" looks about right.'

'Okay.' The chairman smiled, picked up his pen, put a tick on the page and initialled it. With that, the top of the pen started to glow golden. 'How about that? I think I'm all out of ink.'

Al stepped forward. 'I'll fix that right away, sir.'

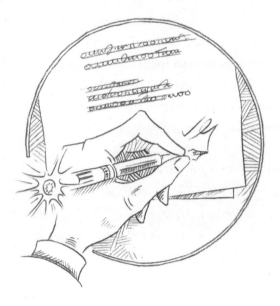

The man handed him the pen and looked down at his notes for the next agenda item. Lexi ignored the coffee and the water, and moved straight to the door. Light from the '& more' button on top of the pen pulsed across Al's hand, but no one other than Lexi seemed to notice it.

He followed her out to the corridor and into the empty office opposite. He turned around and she reached into his bag and took out the activated peg.

'Five of them?' she said. 'There are five of them?'

Doug blinked at her and scrunched himself into the shadows in case he was in trouble.

'Yep. I asked for one with five, 'cause I thought the ones with three and four were getting a bit easy.' Al touched the button and the top of the pen opened up as if it was melting.

'Not my fault, Lex. And in two seconds there'll be only four of them, anyway.'

He held the pen out to her.

'I know it's not your fault. It's just—' They had four more chances to find Grandad Al, four more chances to get lost.

She pushed the peg into the portal.

$\mathcal{T}$HEY SHUDDERED OVER more small bumps, and again the drop was short.

The mist cleared and below them was an island, or in fact several islands and the broken coastline at the edge of a continent. The island they were falling towards was taken up by a city, with its grid of streets crammed with reddish-brown buildings several storeys high. There were steamships and sailing ships at work on the water.

'Wings!' Lexi shouted as they dropped towards a street crowded with carriages and carts. 'Traffic!'

Al panicked and flapped his arms and tumbled. Lexi swung hers out from her sides and swerved. Just in time, Al did the same.

There was a park on one side of the street and they aimed for the grass, but only made it as far as a roadside tree.

Al dropped through the leaves and ended up straddling a branch. 'Whoa! Nearly 19th-century roadkill.' The steamboats said 19th century, and the carriages looked right for it, too.

Lexi was caught in a pile of skirts in the fork of the tree's two biggest branches. She couldn't even work out how many layers she was wearing.

Al laughed. 'You look like a doll, like the kind of doll some nannas hide their toilet rolls under.'

'Oh yeah?' She struggled to move. 'You've got your pants tucked into your socks.'

Al didn't care. She was right – his pants were weirdly baggy above the knees and tucked into long socks below them – but this time he was the winner. He wasn't wearing leggings or looking like a way to hide toilet paper. He mostly looked as he had in 1929.

'Just get the peg out,' Lexi said as she pushed herself up and lifted her boot over the fork. A squirrel dropped out from between two of her petticoats, shook its head and dashed up the tree trunk.

She half-jumped, half-slipped to the ground, leaving a torn piece of petticoat behind her on the branch. How did anyone do anything dressed like this? Or maybe you weren't supposed to. Al's bag was made of leather this time, and he took it off and handed it down to her, before swinging his leg over the branch and dropping easily to the ground.

'That last one was quick,' Lexi said as she undid the buckle. 'We didn't even get to street level. How would we have found Grandad Al if it had been the right era?'

'I don't know.' Al realised there was a lot he didn't know, a lot they didn't think to ask Caractacus when they met him in the 5th century. 'I didn't think it'd work out so easily.'

Lexi had the peg in her hand and she showed him. 'Still America. Closer to the 1830s, though. New York before skyscrapers. When did they get those?'

Through the park, Al could see a grand building with columns and a domed tower. Across the street was an office

43

block five storeys high with a sign on it that, in curly old-fashioned writing, said 'The New York Times'. 'There's nothing higher than that.' He pointed to it. 'I think they have to invent the lift before buildings get much bigger. That's got to happen some time around now.'

'It's 30 years after Nantucket.' She ran her finger over the writing that glowed on the peg. 'What do you think?'

'1865? The Civil War's over, or about to be. And it wasn't, or isn't, near here anyway. I don't think this is the one for Nantucket, though. I think we'll get closer. We've got four more pegs and it's "okay". The word "okay". It's not going to go back to the year 12 in the next step. It's a very American word.'

'You don't know that.' She put the peg back in the bag. 'After this, we could go straight to Africa 300 years ago. You don't know any more than I do. What about the 30-year window?'

'It goes for 30 years.' Al took the bag and put it back on. 'I hoped we'd get closer than this. He could go anywhere in 30 years. He was a word hunter for a lot longer than we've been. He hunted a lot of words. He might know better places to go in the 1860s than Nantucket. It's not very far from here, but it's not right next door, either. We don't know what would happen to the portal – or anything else – if we made a side-trip. And it could take days.'

'The stupid 30-year window was your idea!' She shouted it at him. She had plenty more to say, but she stopped herself. Thirty years was a long time. '"Okay." We're waiting for someone to do something relevant to the history of "okay". And if the next step is Germania and some stupid battle and we've overshot by 2,000 years because of you, I am taking the pegs and I'm going home alone.'

'It's not going to be. We checked. Mursili checked.' The choice *not* to go to Nantucket now was a risk and Al knew it – Grandad Al might be there and they mightn't get a better chance – but *going* to Nantucket might be a bigger one. Everything was a risk, even when no one was shooting arrows at you.

A sign beside the path identified the building through the park as City Hall. It seemed like an obvious place to start.

They followed the path past garden beds to the part of the building that looked most likely to have the front door.

There were steps leading up to stone columns that supported a balcony.

As they got closer, two guards appeared between the columns.

'What's our excuse for being here?' Al realised they hadn't sorted that out yet. 'What do we say to them?'

'Sorry, folks. Not today,' one of the guards called out. 'We're still shut down after the president's funeral procession. Not much open around here but the *Times*.' He pointed back across the park.

'We've just come to pay our respects,' Al said. He had heard people use the phrase in movies.

'Well, the train's halfway to Illinois by now, but we have condolence books.' The guard seemed to be indicating something behind him that they couldn't see. 'You'd be welcome to step inside and add your names.'

They climbed the steps and found that the first set of doors to the building was open, though there were doors closed beyond them. In the alcove were two desks, each with an open leather-bound book and a pen.

'Maybe we'll find "okay" in them,' Lexi said as she opened one. 'Or at least word-hunter initials.'

Al checked the other book. He flicked through page after page, but there were no 'okay's or initials. Each page had a column of names running down its left side and then a wider column for comments. In fine, elegant writing, one New Yorker after another had written about their shock and sense of loss at the death of President Lincoln.

He turned around to Lexi. 'I only kind of knew it as a historical event. Not as something that mattered to people. That they took so personally.'

Lincoln had been alive, and then shot, and then dead. He wasn't to these people a marble giant in a monument or a face on Mount Rushmore. He wasn't any part of history. He had lived in their present and worked to change it.

'You were the Washington of our time,' one visitor had written, starting to find him his place in history. 'A true leader, who made us a better people of a better country.'

'What's this?' Lexi said. She pointed to an entry in her book which read 'John Buck 13'.

Al had no idea.

He took it to the guard, who said, 'Oh, 13.' He seemed to be trying to remember John Buck. 'I think that man was a slave. He'd once been a slave. Now he's free. We haven't changed the Constitution in 60 years, but the 13th Amendment will be the one that makes sure no one in this country is ever a slave again. He probably couldn't write, John Buck. Just his name and numbers. That's what he's thanking the president for. Thirteen. The president got it through Congress two months ago.'

It was almost impossible to believe, in this city with wide streets and street lamps and carriages, grand stone buildings and rich Americans, that people had kept slaves – that some people *were* slaves – in the same country, and very recently. Al didn't know what to say to the guard, so he just nodded and said, 'Thanks.'

He took the book back to the table, picked up the pen and wrote 'Alastair Hunter', and in the comments column he put '13'. Lexi did the same.

As they walked out and down the steps, a cool breeze blew down Park Row, caught the new green leaves in the trees and made their branches sway. It was early spring. They didn't speak until they reached the street.

'The hard thing is,' Lexi said, 'that this bit of the past doesn't look so past. If it was people running round with axes, I guess the idea of slaves – well, it'd never be right, but it'd be less of a shock. But the idea that someone with a fur coat and a watch and books that I've read could *own* people—'

'Not anymore, though.' Al stopped to watch a carriage go past. 'It had to change, and this is when it did.' Doug moved around in his bag and the pegs clanked together. 'Nothing to do with "okay" over there, though – not that I could see.'

'Not much open around here but the *Times*.' Lexi was looking across the road, to the *New York Times* building. 'A newspaper worked for us last time. Maybe that's where we should have gone. We might have missed it. What if we have?'

'We can't – Don't even think that. I might be a copy boy again. This could be it.' Al took another look at Lexi. 'You're richer than last time, maybe. I don't know. I can't work this one out. My head's still spinning a bit with the Lincoln stuff. Let's just go.'

They crossed the road. There was a security guard in the foyer, so they waited outside. It had been easier in Chicago. They'd just appeared on the top floor of the building and gone nowhere near security. Al figured they had one chance with the guard. They needed a good story – one to get them both into the building, not just him as a copy boy – and they didn't have it yet.

Lexi focused on the conversations of men coming in and going out. Most were about Lincoln – the shooting was recent – but others were about baseball and girls. No one said 'okay' – not once.

She kicked a piece of chalk that had been left on the ground, and it skidded across something that looked like a hopscotch game. Some of the lines weren't where she expected, though. As she tried to work it out, she saw the initials 'WH' and 'TH' where the numbers 8 and 9 should have been. She grabbed Al's sleeve and showed him.

'And there's the chalk,' she said, pointing to it. 'It's like they were just here. Right here, outside the building.'

Al glanced along the street. No one was watching them. No one he could see was wearing a key badge.

'There's no "AH".' Lexi was still focused on the chalk writing. 'No Grandad Al.'

'Maybe he didn't do this one. Or maybe he wasn't doing initials when he was here. He used a pen, anyway. A blue ballpoint.' But the chalk was right there. He would have picked it up and added his initials, if he'd been there.

Lexi picked up the chalk, wiped the 7 away and put 'LH' and, next to it, 'AH'.

'We're on track for the word, though,' she said as she set the chalk down on the 6. 'That's something. The others came through here. I just hope we're not too late.'

Two men stopped near them on their way into the building.

'I'm not at all sure about this,' the older one said. He had a dark coat, and grey hair. 'People are still buying Pearline and the new soap isn't doing so well.'

'This'll change that, Mr Pyle. Another spread in the *Times*.' The younger man took a step towards the entrance, but Mr Pyle didn't move, so he stopped again. 'I don't think we pushed it hard enough before. It's time for the big push now. I think the name is right. It's a new word. It's fresh. It's very American.'

Lexi and Al looked at each other.

'Perhaps you should try it out on us,' Lexi called out, before they could go inside.

The two men stopped and turned.

'Are you talking to me, child?' Mr Pyle straightened his shoulders and made himself stand taller. 'What do you mean, try it out on you?'

'A fresh new name. Who better to try it out on than someone who'll give you a fresh new opinion?' Lexi knew she needed more. Mr Pyle wasn't going to hang around talking to a random 12-year-old on a street. 'I'm Alexandra. My father's one of the editors of the *Times*.'

'The man who – yet again – wants to sell me space to advertise my soap? I'd hardly call you independent.' Mr Pyle laughed. 'But all right. You can tell me what you think. We've got a few minutes to spare.' He reached into his coat and fumbled around in a deep pocket. 'Mr Austin, do tell this young lady what you have in mind.' He pulled out a bar of soap. It was wrapped in paper with its name in red inside a decorative black border.

'OK soap,' Mr Austin said, hoping she would like it. His job was riding on the success of OK soap, and pitching to the young lady really wasn't part of his plan. 'No one used OK as a product name before Mr Pyle started to a couple of years ago. He put it in the *Times* then – just to test the water – and I'm certain that a full campaign will be all it takes to make it popular. More and more people are taking a liking to soap, and we think OK is where soap is heading in the '60s.' The look he gave her was almost pleading. Young ladies could be so hard to please, and his plans could fall apart right here on the steps if she didn't like the sound of them. 'Soon enough, when any of us says "OK", we'll be thinking soap. This soap.'

Mr Pyle handed the soap to Lexi. Already the 'O' in 'OK' had become a glowing gold button.

'Why not?' she said. 'I think you're right. I like the way this looks. I could see my mother buying it tomorrow. I like the idea of OK soap.' She held it up to her nose and sniffed. She wanted to say something good about the fragrance, but it didn't smell of much at all. 'In fact, I like it enough that I don't want to give it back.'

Mr Pyle laughed again. 'Do you do this for everyone your father's selling column space to? Wait on the steps and win them over, so all he has to do is ink the deal? You're good, young lady. You're welcome to keep it. I don't need two members of the same family holding a block of my

soap and telling me what a treasure it is.' He laughed again.
'Mr Austin, let's go buy a piece of the front page.'

As soon as they were safely around the street corner, Al went
to open his backpack, but Lexi stopped him.

'How long have we got, do you think?' she said. 'I agree
we don't go to Nantucket now. But, if we were going to go,
how long would we have?'

'But we're not going to go.' He wasn't following her
point.

'One time, though – maybe next time – we will. And
how long will the portal be there? How long do they stay
like this? We normally open them in a few seconds, and once

they're open we go. But if we keep this one and don't open it, how long will it last?'

'Another question for Caractacus.' Al undid the buckles on his pack and found the activated peg.

'Even if it's not this time, this word could be our best chance for Nantucket in the late 1830s. There's no Caractacus between now and then. We've got to work this out ourselves, and this is one of those rare times that someone isn't trying to massacre us with an axe when we've got to the portal.'

'Okay.' His instinct was still to touch the portal and then shove a peg into it. That had always been the thing to do before.

'Mostly, the thing that creates the portal – the thing someone says and that we need to hear – comes along soon after we arrive somewhere. Sometimes it's just a few minutes. So, if the next step puts us right here 25 years before now, we couldn't just go straight to Nantucket, because we might miss it. Then we might have nothing. We could be stuck here. I think that, next time, we have to find the word the way we usually do, get the portal and then look for Nantucket. If we know the portal will stay around for long enough.'

'So we don't touch this one just yet?' He fiddled with the levers on the peg and then set it down.

'Exactly. But we've got to be ready to all the time. It takes a few seconds for the glow to fully come on – it should take at least a few seconds to fade. So we have to watch it. And I don't think we can sit staring at it on some coach to Nantucket.'

'It's an island,' he said. 'Nantucket.' Sometimes he wished he could fight the urge to have the last word. 'But a coach'd get us most of the way there, I guess. And it'd be a long trip. And I don't have Caractacus's number handy. Yeah. Let's watch it.'

As their first day of waiting turned into evening and then a cold night, they watched the streets empty and they grew hungry. They hid in the shadow of a doorway and, through the windows of Delmonico's across South William Street, they watched diners in suits and dark dresses eating French food and drinking wine. Al followed every mouthful and invented the flavours until his stomach growled too much. They had found half a bag of nuts hours before, but that was all.

The last customers left and eventually the staff did too, and the restaurant closed.

'They didn't even finish,' Al said as the lights went out. 'Some of those people left food on their plates.'

Lexi was sitting on the ground, holding her knees and taking her turn to watch the glowing 'O' on the soap packet. 'I know we could get out of here just by touching the portal, but we can't crack yet.'

'I'm not saying—' He stopped himself. It wasn't the time to fight. 'I'm not cracking. I'm hungry. There's got to be more food in there.'

'So you're suggesting we break into a restaurant and

steal some food?' Al was ready for her to tell him how wrong it'd be, and then she said, 'How would we get in?'

The front door was never likely to be the answer, and it was bolted shut. The building was a wedge shape, with the door at its point and windows along the sides. Further down the street they found an alley that led somewhere behind the restaurant. Al took out his torch and they made their way past vents and pipes and piles of rubbish to a loading bay.

There was a big double door that seemed to be bolted on the inside, top and bottom, and a smaller door next to it that rattled but was locked.

'I don't think anything could get in here,' Al said. Then he felt a thump in his bag and the scratching of tiny feet. Doug twisted and turned as he poked his head out. 'Anything except a rat, maybe.' Doug climbed up to his shoulder and ran down to his hand. Al set him on the ground. 'Okay, buddy. Think you can get us in there?'

As Lexi watched them, she couldn't believe this was their best shot. 'So he's, what, Doug the Super Rat now? You've been training him in your room? I suppose he also catches bullets in his teeth and drives the getaway car.'

Doug could smell food over the rubbish stink of the alley – pheasant, duck fat, 18 different kinds of cheese. How many kinds of cheese could he eat before he was sick? Twelve at least. And he'd keep the other six for later.

He tracked the waft of food smell to the small door and along the bottom of it. At the hinge end, the base of the door was splintered. He could stick his head through. Cheese,

cheese, duck fat, cheese – the smell was powerful now. He wriggled and pushed and breathed all the way out and tumbled through the hole.

As he fell through, the door rattled and a key slipped from the lock. It clanged like a dropped fork when it landed on the tiles.

'What's happening?'

Doug didn't even notice Al's voice or see the torchlight under the door. He was halfway to the kitchen with his mind on nothing but food stink – vegetable peelings, crispy fried anything, tubs of lard.

Al could see the key glinting in the torchlight. He took a wire coat hanger from his bag, twisted it into shape and hooked the key.

'Genius,' he said as he stood up. 'Super Rat.' He unlocked the door and pushed it open. 'Hand Doug the keys to the getaway car, Lex. I think he's got it covered. And it looks like the coat hanger was useful after all.'

'Yeah, okay.' Lexi had argued with him about it, saying she didn't think they'd get much time to hang clothes. 'You get credit for the coat hanger, but I'm pretty sure Doug's role in that was a total fluke.' She peered down the hallway, but Doug was nowhere to be seen.

They found him in a kitchen bin rolling on some leftover quail.

They lit a gas lamp and ate bread from a basket of rolls and loaf-ends, while they worked out what to cook.

'Still totally fresh.' Al wouldn't have cared how stale it was – he'd never been so hungry in his life. 'They probably bake every day.'

The fridge at home was always full. The next meal was only ever hours away. There was always fruit in the bowl whenever you wanted it. Food was something you could assume would be there. It had scared him, he realised, to be without it. It was worse than the hunger, thinking about food and having no idea when you might find some – or if.

He cooked a huge omelette, while Doug stuck his face in a bowl of congealed duck fat and Lexi kept watching the portal.

They ate all they could and then filled Al's bag with bread and cheese and jars of things that were labelled in French and that they didn't even recognise.

They locked the door on the way out and Al slipped the key back under it, where it would look like it had fallen sometime during the night.

Al took the next shift – two hours or as close as he could make it, staring at the portal, while Lexi slept on some empty sacks. Much of the time he stood with the bar of soap in front of him on a head-high windowsill. He thought about Grandad Al and the old photos and New York in the 1860s and sleep. He particularly thought about sleep. And then his mind snapped back to the portal and to his fear of losing it. He was wide awake again, focused.

They saw the night through in two-hour shifts and caught up on sleep the next day, still one at a time with the other watching the portal.

By the second night, whoever was sleeping dreamt only of the glowing button, blinking, fading, slipping beyond reach.

The OK soap ads appeared the next morning and all that day the portal glowed even brighter.

'It's like jetlag,' Lexi said as she stretched her arms and legs after a sleep.

Al was eating bread and cheese. 'Yeah, I know. I feel like someone could take my appendix out now and I wouldn't notice. I don't think I can go on much longer.'

It was late afternoon.

By nightfall, when that day's edition of *The New York Times* was off the newsstands and there were few new readers for it, the portal started to dim. Then a crack appeared.

'Now,' Lexi said, shaking Al's shoulder. 'We need to go now.'

HERE WAS ANOTHER rush of small bumps and a short straight drop. They fell into another night. There was land below – a dark country at the edge of a black sea. But there were lights too – the soft glow and then clear lines of street lamps, a grid of them, then light spilling from buildings.

They landed in thick warm coats at the edge of a street. Al's was black, Lexi's was light brown with ivory buttons. When she moved, she felt the new leather of her boots creak. There was a mist in the air and it glowed around the lamps.

'I don't think we have to look too far this time.' She pointed to a sign that read 'Brooklyn OK Club, meeting 7 o'clock tonight'. Her hands were in some kind of fur tube and she pulled them out in a panic to check the portal. 'No soap.' She laughed. 'I'm glad that's over.'

A carriage stopped and four people climbed down, then walked up the steps into the building. The men were wearing top hats and the women had furs around their shoulders.

'That looks like what we're dressed for. Let's see when this is.' Al reached for the single silver buckle on his black satchel. When he opened it the leather smelt new. Then Doug burped and it smelt like 14 kinds of cheese. 'The time's good. Really good.' He showed the peg to Lexi.

'This is it, then.' She folded the fur hand warmer and pushed it into her pocket. 'I guess it'll be in there. Or at least that's where we have to start.'

'If we'd stayed longer at City Hall last time, do you think we'd have missed it completely?' It had been bothering Al. 'Does it come up once and, if you're not in the right spot, is that it? Or would there have been another chance when the ads got published? Maybe that was the real chance.'

'I think you might be mistaking me for Caractacus. Put it on the list, if you want.' She didn't want to think about it, or to think that one wrong move could see them stuck. 'Maybe us being there triggers it. But let's go get this one. And let's hope it'll fit in your bag.'

As they crossed the road, she took a closer look at the sign about the meeting. There in the middle of the 'O' of 'OK' she could make out the initials 'WH' and 'TH'. They were on track. There was still no sign of Grandad Al, though. If he hadn't done 'okay', he wouldn't know to head to Brooklyn on this particular night five years after Nantucket. It was too much to hope that he'd be in the crowd. But they were closer at least.

'You're here for OK?' the man on the door said when they reached the top of the steps.

Lexi couldn't believe it was so easy. 'We're definitely here for OK.'

She and Al took a step inside the meeting room and checked for a portal, but nothing showed itself. 'OK' was everywhere, though. A woman passed them each an 'OK'

**BROOKLYN**

**O K**

**CLUB**

MEETING 7 O'CLOCK TONIGHT

ribbon from a box and there were banners on the walls reading 'Vote for OK'. There were wooden chairs set out in rows, most of them with people on them already.

'I'm assuming this isn't all about soap,' Al said.

'Have you noticed how this one keeps being "okay", however you spell it? It's not like "harrow, halloo, hello". I thought it'd change more.' Lexi was starting to wish the rules were the same each time. Or, if they weren't the same, she wished she understood them better. 'I wonder why we had to meet Mr Pyle and find out about his soap?'

'Oh, wonderful,' a man said, looking right at her. He had a medal on the breast of his black coat. 'You *are* the twins, aren't you? The ribbons go here.' He indicated his ribbon, which was on his lapel. 'Do you need to wear those keys? Could the ribbons go over them, perhaps – just for now?' he kept smiling. He didn't seem to need answers. 'I'm Talbot. You'll have been told to look out for Talbot, I assume? Mr Talbot? Follow me.'

It felt as if they had no choice. Al checked the room as they went and he could see Lexi doing the same. It might not be the crazy ancient past, but things had gone wrong before when they'd least expected it.

Mr Talbot took them to the right and along the side of the audience, to steps leading to a door beside the stage. He knocked on it and it opened.

'Oh, the children,' another man's voice said from inside. 'The twins. Thank you, Mr Talbot.'

The door opened fully and Mr Talbot ushered them in. Al could feel himself tensing up. But it was 1840, a meeting house. No one would be here shooting kings or invading or robbing.

'Right,' the new man said, even before the door had closed behind them. 'We're planning to keep the introductions brief – brief, but rousing. We need them in the right frame of mind when the president comes on.' He had a dark moustache, a satchel quite like Al's and a small bunch of flowers in one hand. 'You'll go out as soon as the president has finished speaking.' He passed the flowers to Lexi. 'You'll give him this.' He was staring at the flowers as if they needed to be checked again. 'They're mostly things you could find in your garden. Nice and simple. We think that's the right message.'

He opened his satchel and took out several copies of a document.

'Are they for me?' Al said. He wondered what he might have to do with them.

The man checked the documents and didn't look up. 'Only if you want to be ready for any last-minute questions OK might have about Texas.' He ran his finger further down the page. 'We've reached a settlement with Mexico to deny Texas's request to become part of the United States.'

Lexi and Al glanced around the room, but still nothing was glowing. It was dark backstage and a portal wouldn't have been hard to see. How much 'okay' would there be in 1840 before the portal appeared?

'Andrew Morrell.' The man finally looked up. 'Aide to the president. I'm the one who exchanged letters with your parents. I thought you'd look more alike, but no matter. They might have dressed you more alike. You'll have to take the coats off.'

'Questions OK might have?' Al wanted to get back to that, and away from Andrew Morrell's focus on details that didn't make a lot of sense.

'Yes, OK – the president, Mr Van Buren, Old Kinderhook.' He looked at them both to make sure his point had got through. 'Did your parents tell you nothing? OK. From Kinderhook, New York, where he was born. OK's what we're going with now. OK clubs, OK ribbons. It sounds—' He paused, to find the right word. 'Affectionate, like the right kind of name for a man of the people. We need to undo all the talk going around about him hosting huge banquets for European ministers when money was tight in '37. They're wrong about him, you know. He wears the finest suits to be found in Manhattan, but they're all bought from his own pocket.'

It was politics, Lexi realised. As their parents often said in the 21st century, politics should have been about big things, but too often it was about how wrong your dress was or how your hair was cut.

'Is that how OK started?' Al asked him. It felt unusual to say something so direct, but he couldn't see why he shouldn't. 'You came up with it for this campaign?'

'I think it is. I think we started it. Or one of the others saw it in a newspaper.' He looked around, as if whoever saw it might be nearby. 'Yes, that was it. It was the *Boston Morning Post*, sometime last year. It was that game they were playing, printing expressions with the wrong initials and spelling, as if they'd been written by people who didn't know better. It's ours now, though. Whenever people think OK, it's the president they'll be thinking of.' Suddenly he stopped and ignored them completely. 'Mr President—'

'Andrew.' An older man stepped forward and stood beside Al, though he didn't seem to notice him. The top of his head was a bald dome, with grey woolly hair sprouting from the sides, and mutton-chop whiskers. He had a top hat in one hand and an elegant cane in the other. 'You have that bill ready for me?'

'Yes, sir.'

Andrew Morrell turned the documents so that the president could see them.

As he took the pen that Andrew Morrell offered him, the president seemed to see Lexi and Al for the first time.

'You're the children who come on at the end.' He had an accent that wasn't quite American. 'You're – what is it – a symbol of our future? Try not to make me look too much like an old man.' He smiled. 'So, how do you see our future?'

'I think—' Al wasn't sure if he was brave enough to tell a president what to do, but he had to give it a try. 'I think you should end slavery now.'

Al knew there was a war to come if it didn't happen, and President Lincoln would be shot at the end of it. In the meantime slaves in some places would be slaves for another quarter of a century. He couldn't guess how different the United States or the world might be if the change came now, in 1840, and it didn't take a war. Or maybe the war in 1840 would be worse. Maybe the slave states would win.

The president smiled again, and nodded. 'I'm sure you know I have a moral objection to it, and that will not shift. I have never kept slaves and I never will. But our Constitution appears to allow it, and there are states that see themselves dependent on it. States have rights. I can't make laws that trample on those rights.'

'What about amending the Constitution?' Al knew it could happen, because one day it would.

'Amending the Constitution? Do you know what that

would take? Become a lawyer, young man, and then a senator and then a better president than I dare to be, and maybe you'll talk those southern states around, but I don't see it being an easy matter.' He looked down at the documents again. 'It's good to have high ideals, though. Don't lose those.' He paused before signing. 'This is Texas?'

'Yes, sir,' Andrew Morrell said. 'This is Texas. If you'd be so good as to put your name to it, give it the OK—'

The moment the president signed the first copy, the 'a' in Van Buren turned into an '& more' button and started to glow. Andrew Morrell lifted the page away for the president to sign the next one. The button glowed against his white shirt front.

Al wanted a distraction, a chance to grab the page and run.

'Sir,' Lexi said. 'It's wrong of me to interrupt, but you were right about my brother. He has his heart set on becoming a lawyer and I know he'd be forever grateful if you allowed him a few minutes to read that first bill you've just signed.'

'Why not?' The president looked flattered. 'He's a bright boy. Why not?'

Andrew Morrell took the document and passed it to Al. He seemed less happy about the idea. 'You're not to leave this room with it. There's light over there.' He nodded in the direction of door that had a lamp next to it. 'Just a few minutes, though. We'll be starting soon.'

Al thanked him and took it. He and Lexi moved over to the door.

'I bet it leads outside,' she said. 'We've probably got two days to get to Nantucket with this. It doesn't matter if they lose it. They've got more copies, and surely Texas becomes part of America, anyway. Doesn't it?'

'But the next step's Boston.' Al put his hand up to stop her opening the door. 'Boston in 1839. We already know that. Andrew Morrell said. Boston's much closer to Nantucket. I googled it. Nantucket's an island. Boston in 1839 – we won't get much better than that.'

'How much closer?' She was looking back towards the president. She wasn't convinced yet. Andrew Morrell was looking their way, as if they couldn't be trusted.

'Less than half as far. And a year closer. It's got to be the place.'

'Okay.'

She turned him to face the light, so that it would look as if he was reading. She reached into his backpack for the peg.

1839

Boston
USA

MACROPHOTOMATIC

IT WAS LIKE falling through a doorway, hardly a stumble before they were out of the cloud and dropping into cold fresh air and a bright day.

There were ships moving in and out of the harbour and red-brick buildings packed in tight near the city centre, right up to the edge of a large park. Lexi and Al were heading for the streets though, and they landed in front of a church. It had a tower with clocks on each side and a steeple rising from the top.

'If this is Boston, I guess we're looking for the *Morning Post*,' Lexi said. She scanned the shopfronts across the road. 'The name'll be on the building, won't it? Newspapers seem to do that.' She checked to see what Al was wearing. 'I think you're a copy boy again, the 1839 version. You keep getting that.'

'Which is a shame, since I've got my heart set on becoming a lawyer.' He laughed, which was something he couldn't do when she said it to President Van Buren.

'Hey, I've read books from this century. That's how they talk.'

She was wearing a bonnet, a jacket with fine stripes and again multiple skirts. She looked to Al like someone who would talk just that way, like the kind of girl who, in period films, turns pale and faints. Her key badge was on her jacket, and he checked to see that his was where it should be, too.

She signalled for him to turn around and started to open the top of his duffel bag. As the air rushed in, Doug smelt the sea, rubbish in a nearby alley, clam chowder.

'Andrew Morrell was *expecting twins*.' It hadn't clicked with Al at the time. 'How does that work? Word hunters can't all be twins, can they? Grandad Al didn't have a twin.'

'Maybe only twins get "okay".' She reached down inside the duffel bag. The activated peg was buried among all the gear they'd brought. 'Or maybe it's what Caractacus said about the dictionary adapting. It could be different if you're by yourself.' She pulled the peg out. 'Yep, this is Boston in 1839. Which means we've got a newspaper to find. And then Grandad Al.'

Two women had stopped to talk on the corner of the street and Lexi walked right up to them.

'Excuse me,' she said. 'We're looking for the offices of the *Boston Morning Post*.'

'Oh, yes.' One of the women had a parasol and she used it to point down the street that ran along the side of the church. 'You're two blocks away. You'll find them on Congress Street.'

They followed her directions, past the church, a shoemaker and a butcher. When they reached Congress Street, they saw an office building with the signs of several businesses on it. One of them was the *Boston Morning Post*. It wasn't the big deal of the *New York Times* building of 1865, with men in uniform on the door and five floors all working on the paper.

They walked into an empty foyer where a board with a list of businesses told them the *Post* was on the third floor. Four letters – a 'W', a 'T' and two 'H's – had been taken from the name of another business, the Boston and Hartford Whaling Company, and rearranged nearby. 'WH', 'TH'. Tucked behind the 'W' was a small scrap of paper – the torn corner of a bus ticket.

'Brilliant,' Al said. 'No buses in 1839, but if you've never seen a bus ticket it's just a piece of thick paper with "Fulham" on it. So, "WH" is probably from the 20th century. If there were more "H"s—' He wanted to add their names.

'There are, in other names up there. But maybe we should focus on the job, rather than plundering the sign.'

Lexi was right. Two sets of initials had been enough for them, and would be enough for any future word hunters as well.

She glanced around the foyer and groaned. 'No lifts. You'd think they could have invented lifts before making buildings like this.' She walked over to the stairs and stopped. 'They could at least have invented better clothes for girls.' She grabbed her skirts, lifted them above her ankles and clumped up the first flight of stairs. 'I can't even see where my feet are going.'

When they reached the third floor, they listened for the sound of typewriters and the clamour of a newspaper office, but all they could hear was a conversation coming from an office down the hall.

'Charles,' one man said, 'it's a fine piece of writing and you know I find it amusing. I wonder, though, about the part where you refer to the Providence editor and say, "If he comes this way he'll need to have his contribution box o.k.". I didn't pick up what "o.k." was at the start, and I think I'm a good test. Perhaps we should gloss it. Let's try it with "all correct" between a couple of dashes after the "o.k.".'

The hall was dimly lit, and Lexi wondered if she could see a glow coming through the open office door at the mention of the word. She and Al were standing in a kind of entrance area, which had two leather sofas and a large polished wooden desk with turned legs. On the desk they could see several folded copies of the *Boston Morning Post* dated Tuesday March 19, 1839. There was an inkwell sunk into the desk at the side near the wall, a cup next to it containing metal rods that must have been pens, and a bell sitting in one corner.

'The readers love it, though,' the man who must have

been Charles said. 'They love the bumpkin spelling and all the initials. They've loved it since last summer and they're always waiting for what we do next.'

'EN – Eye no. I can play around with bumpkin spelling too and I know readers love it. That's not the point.'

A chair scraped across the floor. Lexi and Al ducked into the stairwell as the men came out of the office and stopped at the desk. The taller man had a sheet of paper in one hand. A pulse of light was coming from near the bottom.

'I'm planning to run it on Saturday,' he said. From the sound of his voice, he was Charles.

'The back page?'

'That's right.' Charles put the paper down on the desk, picked up one of the pens and dipped it into the ink. 'We should change these, too.' He pointed to the newspapers on the desk. 'Yesterday's papers are old news already. We should get a boy to bring up a few copies of today's.'

He circled the date on the top paper with his pen and wrote something next to it in capitals. Then he turned back to his article.

'Gloss it in?' he said, and the other man nodded. 'All right. "O-K dash all correct." Happy now?'

'IK – ixtremely kontent.'

Charles laughed, set the sheet down on the pile of newspapers and rang the bell.

'Where is that boy?' he said as they walked back down the hall. 'We should fix a bell to ring in the basement, since he's down there boxing type whenever Joe'll let him.'

Lexi and Al moved back to the desk as quietly as they could. Down the hall, they heard an office door close.

'What was that about the boy boxing in the basement?' Lexi hadn't expected boxing at a newspaper.

'Boxing type. I think it's when they take all the metal letters and set up the pages for printing.' It was the best answer Al could manage without access to Google. 'Okay, it's Wednesday today.' He checked the date on the newspapers again. Charles had written 'TODAY'S PLEASE!' 'The 20th. If it's like the ad in *The New York Times*, we've got until Saturday evening.'

Lexi picked up the handwritten article. 'It's really there. It's a joke spelling. "Okay" started off as a joke. Oll korrect.' The 'o' of 'o.k.' had turned into a glowing '& more' button. 'But if we take this, maybe it won't get published. It looks like it's the only copy. It's different from 1929, when they typed it and did about six of them. Remember that copy boy pulling the copies apart?'

'If we take it and bring it back—'

'Then it might not be published on Saturday. The whole word might not—'

Someone was coming up the stairs.

'Sit down,' Al whispered. 'Pretend we're here for something else. Hide the article.'

They sat on one of the sofas, and Lexi folded the article to protect the portal and tucked it behind her. A boy around their age appeared at the top of the stairs in no great hurry. He stopped when he saw them there.

'You folks been attended to?' he said.

'We're here to see Charles,' Lexi told him. 'We're cousins on his mother's side. We're early. He knows we're here.'

The boy nodded and checked the desk. He read Charles's note on the top copy of the paper, and he picked the papers up.

'Sorry.' He adjusted the papers in his arms so that he could carry them all. 'It should have been today's. My fault. I'll go get some now, hot off the press.'

Still not hurrying, he walked back to the stairs, leaving Lexi and Al alone in the room. Lexi pulled the article out from behind her and unfolded it. The portal was still glowing.

'This is killing me,' Al said. 'We've got it already. That should be the hard bit. Grandad Al could be out there somewhere. We're so close. But we can't take it.'

'Let's copy it. Charles rang the bell for that guy to take the article, and he'll be back with new newspapers. We can copy it and he can take the copy.'

She stood up, walked over to the desk and pulled open its two drawers. One of them had paper in it. She lifted a sheet out and held it up.

'Good one,' Al said. 'I'm pretty sure your writing's better than mine.'

She took a close look at Charles's article and the way he formed his letters. She copied them as well as she could, all the time being careful not to touch the portal. She even fixed up the messy part where he had added 'all correct'.

The article was in Al's duffel bag and they were sitting down again just as the boy came back with a pile of the day's papers.

'Charles just brought that out for you,' Lexi said, pointing to the sheet of paper.

The boy picked it up and glanced at it. He didn't seem particularly interested.

'Before you go,' Al said, as the boy turned for the stairs, 'we're just passing through Boston – we're actually heading for Nantucket, but we haven't made all our travel arrangements. What do you think would be our best way to get there?'

'Nantucket? I can't imagine why – I'm sure you have your reasons.' He thought about it. 'You could try the docks. There must be ships coming in from Nantucket from time to time.' It didn't sound promising. 'Or you could take a coach to the Cape, to Barnstable, then ask around there for the best place to sail from. Maybe South Yarmouth. The coach station's on Milk Street, in the direction of the harbour. I think that's what I'd do. If I had the time, money and inclination to go to Nantucket.'

'The money,' Lexi said once he had gone again. 'What do we do to get the money?'

Al already had a plan. 'We sell papers.'

They picked up every copy the boy had left and carried them quietly down the stairs. Lexi was worried it was stealing, but Al said they were left there to be given away anyway, to anyone visiting the *Post*. Even if it was stealing, he was going to take them. They needed to find their grandfather.

They left the building and turned into Milk Street. The coach station was easy to find. They checked the boards listing departures, and found one headed 'Cape Cod' that included Barnstable as a stop on the way to Provincetown. It was leaving in half an hour. That was all the time they had to sell as many papers as possible.

They walked around the station, selling to people about to depart and, when a coach arrived, they made sure they were standing nearby as people climbed out.

'*Morning Post*, hot off the press,' Al called out, holding up a folded copy. 'Welcome to Boston.'

It seemed to be a service people liked and the last paper was gone by the time the next coach was empty. When Al added the coins in his pockets to the money in Lexi's bonnet, it was quite a weight in his hands. It felt like a lot of money. He counted it up, and was less positive.

'Three dollars ten.' It was a lot of coins for three dollars ten. 'Do you think two people can get to Nantucket for that?'

It turned out they couldn't, not even in 1839. The driver of the Cape Cod coach looked at the coins in their hands and laughed.

'But we really have to get there,' Lexi said. And then further. It was all looking too hard. 'You can have my boots instead. What about that? They're good boots. They're almost new.'

She lifted her skirts a little and he took a step back.

'They're not my size.' He blocked his view of her ankles with his hand, but took a careful look at the boots. 'I could get a good price for them, though. You're right – they are good boots.'

'It's a deal,' she said, before he could tell her it wasn't.

So they rode on the coach to Barnstable for the price of a pair of good used boots. Lexi sat with her socked feet showing beneath her skirts, and their fellow passengers all looking the other way. Next they could sell Al's boots and her jacket if they had to, and they still had three dollars ten.

'I keep imagining him in that daggy orange towelling hat,' Lexi said as they passed through Weymouth. 'And holding a fish.' She tried to picture a 19th-century Grandad

Al – the man gone missing from 30 years of family photos, four years older now than when he left and wearing a black narrow-waisted coat and dark cravat, like the men in the carriage.

The coach stopped in every small town, but only for as long as it took to allow people to get on and off. It moved slowly, though. Al wanted Google so he could find a map and work out how long the journey would take. In Plymouth the driver called a longer break. Everyone got off the coach to walk around. Those who hadn't brought food went to buy some. There was soup being sold with crusty bread, and Doug poked his nose most of the way out of the duffel bag before Al shook the bag and he dropped back inside.

They were all hungry, but Lexi and Al didn't know when they would need their money. Al tried to think about other things, which meant he had five minutes thinking about a hundred different kinds of great food, before he reminded himself this was all about Grandad Al. It would be worth it if they could find him.

Lexi could feel the cold ground through her socks and her feet were going numb. They walked back to the small coach house, where passengers came and went. As they sat on a bench waiting to be called to board, Lexi realised a man was staring at her.

She nudged Al and said, 'Opposite corner, near the door.'

When Al turned to look at him, the man's eyes opened wide. He stood up to walk across to them, and tripped over someone else's bag. He hardly seemed to notice. He pushed past two people and stepped up onto a bench and off the other side.

Al put his duffel bag on his back. He and Lexi got to their feet and started to back away.

'No, please,' the man said. He stopped. He looked desperate. 'Please.'

It was a crowded room. They were safe enough.

He grabbed his collar and held it out to show them. That was when they saw the peg key he'd pinned there.

'Grandad Al—' Lexi reached out to Al's shoulder to steady herself. The man had wavy brown hair. He was thin and tall. Their grandfather hadn't looked like that in the photos. He was grinning, pushing the key on his collar out with his thumb.

'Will Hunter,' he said as he reached them, holding his hand out to shake theirs. 'Did Caractacus send you?'


It wasn't Grandad Al. Will Hunter was 15 in London in early 1918, when he found the *Curious Dictionary*. He had had it for nine months before his turn hunting 'Hello' came. It had been Lexi and Al's first word, but he had done dozens by then. He had passed safely through the first step in Menlo Park, New Jersey, to the whaler off Nantucket, but the portal had gone to another ship in the fog. He had seen the light and had almost been able to reach it. He had called out, but too late.

It was Will Hunter they had blocked at the portal, not Grandad Al.

Lexi stared at the rough wooden floor of the coach house and tried not to cry. They had saved a hunter and that was a good thing. But they had used up their only clue in the search for Grandad Al. He was in some other part of the past, and the past went on for thousands of years. She wanted to shout at Caractacus and demand whatever magic it would take – or knowledge, or whatever stupid thing he wanted to call it – to give her time with the grandfather she had never met.

At first Will had worked mostly on whalers, in case 'hello' came up again.

'But that was one word,' he said, 'and I'd already missed it. Every night, the crew were looking into the dark for whales and I was looking for a tiny light. And thinking all the time about other words – words I'd done and words I hadn't – and where I might need to be, and when. New York's a better bet than Nantucket. That's where I've been, mostly. I've been back in Nantucket the past few weeks, since I can earn good money there, but I'm actually on my way to Boston. If I remember correctly, "okay" is about to go through there.'

Al laughed. 'We've got "okay" in my bag.'

Will blinked. 'The article? You've got the article before they published it?' He wiped his eyes with the back of his hand. 'I was sure I only landed there when the article came out, and that's not until Saturday. When are you from? Why are you here in Plymouth?'

'We knew someone got lost in Nantucket.' It was the best way Lexi could put it.

'So Caractacus did send you.' He took a deep breath, and let himself smile. 'I lost my pegs. Someone stole them from me. I was sleeping in a park. I didn't know if they'd work for other words or words that I'd done before, but I never got to try. What's the plan? Have you got pegs for me? Do I get to go home or—'

'You will,' Al said. It was what Will needed to hear. 'Not straightaway, but you will. For now you'll come with us. Then we'll either pass close to 1918 or more likely go back

to Caractacus. He can get you home from there.' Al hoped it
was true.

Will nodded. However much he'd thought about this
moment, it was a lot to take in. 'I don't even know how the
war's going.'

'You win. We win. It finishes in 1918.' Al couldn't bring
himself to say that another world war would come along in
just over 20 years.

Will took a handkerchief from his pocket and blew his
nose into it. 'Good. It's such a relief to hear it. My brother—'
He scrunched the handkerchief up and rubbed his eyes with
his sleeve. 'It needed to finish.'

A bell rang. The coach to the Cape was about to leave,
but there was no longer any reason to be on it.

'I'm keeping the boots,' the coach driver said to Lexi. 'We had a deal.'

The word hunters left the coach house and walked out to the road. Will laughed as he watched the world of 1839 going on. He had been lost and robbed and now he had his ticket out. He was too happy to notice Lexi gazing blankly at the ground, wanting him to be someone else and wondering how many battles she might have to fight in the huge blank past, and whether Grandad Al would be at the end of any of them.

'Let's go down here,' Will said, and led them into a side street.

Al checked the two pegs in his bag and took out the one that had activated. He opened the folded article and the portal shone brightly.

'Next step's easy,' Will said. 'You'll be back home before you know it. Do you mind if I—'

He reached forward and touched the portal.

THIS TIME THEY veered sideways, then felt blood rush to their heads as they slowed down. It was a longer drop – far longer than the others for 'okay'. There was a bump as they tumbled from fog into a clear sky.

Lexi and Al recognised the shape of the land below. It was New York again, but there was no New York. They were falling to the north, towards a river – towards a single wooden ship under sail.

'Crow's nest,' Will called out. 'Top of the mast.'

It took a small correction to their fall, but a precise one. Will and Lexi landed cleanly in the empty crow's nest, but Al clipped the edge and tipped over it face first. By the time he stopped moving there was a hat jammed over his eyes.

He heard Lexi say, 'And the prize for best comedy landing goes to—' When he pulled the hat off, it was no surprise to see that she was pointing at him.

'If the two of you had left any room—' It was the best excuse he could manage.

All three of them were dressed as crew, with puffy shirts and pants with a snug fit that, from Al's point of view, made them too much like leggings. As if the landing wasn't bad enough. Luckily Lexi seemed more focused on Will this time.

As he reached into his bag for the peg, Will stopped him.

'This'll be easy. I've done it before and I know exactly where we need to be.' He pointed down to the stern.

'But why are we here at all?' Lexi seemed less troubled by the swaying of the crow's nest than Al. Even a small movement down on the ship meant a lot of movement up here. 'Surely the job's done. "Okay" doesn't go any further into the past than 1839.'

'Fair question.' Will reached back to grab the edge of the crow's nest as it swayed the other way. 'It didn't take much to start "okay", but it took a lot to keep it going. It might have died out if they hadn't used it as a soap name, for instance. And for it to last until the soap came along, Van Buren had to be Old Kinderhook. And for that he needed to have been born in Kinderhook. So welcome to the early 1600s, where we might just find out how that came about. The man on that raised deck in the high boots and fancy collar is Henry Hudson. He's English, but working for the Dutch East India Company. They're exploring the river. The ship's called the *Half Moon*. One day they'll name the river after him. He doesn't know that, and he doesn't know he'll disappear in two years' time, searching for the Northwest Passage. I looked him up in *Encyclopaedia Britannica* after I got home. Do you do that?'

'Something like it,' Lexi said. 'Wait till you see.'

'The deck's called an aftercastle. That's where we need to be. The one at the front's a forecastle.' Will could picture the illustrations in the encyclopedia, a portrait of Hudson next to an engraving of the *Half Moon* – *Halve Maen* in Dutch – with Mohican canoes approaching from the shore. Hudson hardly looked like the portrait at all, but the *Half Moon* was close enough.

'So why exactly are we up here and not down there?' Al was feeling queasy and could have done without the lesson in ship parts. He already knew all that.

'Another fair question. Take a look at the top of the cliffs.' Will searched until he could find the exact spot, and then pointed. There were children crouched in the long grass and staring down at the deck of the ship. 'We wouldn't have the "k" in "okay" if it wasn't for them. Let's go to the aftercastle and watch it happen.'

He led the way down the rope ladder, and when they reached the deck he said, 'Pick up a rope or something and look like you know how to use it.'

Lexi found a mallet lying next to some wooden pins. It was only once it was in her hand that she realised she could use it as a weapon if she needed to. 'Okay' had been a relief from that point of view – no battles, no threats to their lives so far. She checked the crew. There were no weapons in sight. She should have made sure of that earlier from the crow's nest, but Will seemed so confident she'd stopped thinking that way.

As they reached the rear deck, they saw Henry Hudson wave to the cliff-top and the children ducked down out of sight. One by one, they cautiously stood up again.

'We'll call this bend Children's Corner,' Hudson announced.

The navigator picked up a quill, dipped it in ink and wrote on the chart in front of him. He was mapping the river as they travelled.

'Kinderhoek,' he said. A glow rose from the page, at the tip of his quill.

Will walked straight up to him and said, 'Sir, I've been sent by the second lieutenant. Your sextant has fallen and broken below decks. He thinks it can be repaired, but he'd like you to give instructions.'

'What? How?' The navigator wasn't happy. 'No one should be touching my sextant. It was in my quarters. How—' He was already walking off. He stopped and turned. 'Captain, permission to leave the aftercastle—'

Hudson nodded.

With the navigator gone, Will, Lexi and Al stepped forward to the chart. The 'h', 'o' and 'e' in 'Kinderhoek' were pulsing brightly, with an 'm' fitting among them to make the word 'home'.

'I wonder,' Will said. For a moment, he dared to hope it would mean home for him too.

He picked up the quill and wrote 'x2' next to the initials 'WH' near the corner of the chart. 'TH' had been written just below. He set the quill down, touched the glowing letters in 'Kinderhoek' and the portal opened. Al already had the peg in his hand.

From nowhere, fog rolled up the river and across the deck, and the *Half Moon* shuddered in a wind that wasn't there.

⟡— —⟡

Lexi, Al and Will blew clear of the deck and into the sky. Will laughed. It was his first flight to the future for four years and there had been many days and nights when he had doubted whether he would ever make another.

The pictures of passing time rushed by – railways and revolutions, factories and fishing fleets. As they fell towards Fig Tree Pocket in the 21st century, it was clear there were still three of them. Will wasn't going back to 1918 yet.

They dropped towards the roof of their house and Lexi shouted, 'This way!' and steered past it. They landed in the ferns at the side.

In the dark inside Al's bag, Doug tried to work out which way was up. He smelt creek mud, cut grass and sausages. He was home.

'Not exactly London in the early 20th century,' Will said, looking around. 'That was probably a bit much to hope for. But it's good to be moving again. Great, actually. I can come with you next time, can't I?'

'Every time.' Lexi stood up and brushed dirt off her pants. 'It'll be good to have you there. You look more ready for a fight than we are. Except right now maybe, when you look like some hot skater dude.' She laughed.

'A hot skater dude? We didn't have a lot of those in 1918. As far as I know. Whatever they are.' Will checked what he was wearing, but it didn't help. 'Skater dude' remained a mystery. He had a black Von Dutch cap on, an orange T-shirt with skulls on it and baggy three-quarter pants. 'I'm going to assume it's legal to be one, unless you tell me otherwise.'

Al felt his phone vibrate in his bag and then it started to ring. It was Mursili.

'You're back,' Mursili said. 'Good. I didn't know what I was going to tell people if it went through to the message area. What happened? Was it 19th century? Did you find your grandfather?'

Al watched Will stand up and straighten his cap. Lexi picked a leaf off his shoulder and blushed.

'Pretty much 19th century and no. But we found the guy from Nantucket in the 1830s. We've brought him back with us.'

'What? Another one?' Mursili sounded excited. 'You're bringing everyone from the past to the present, one by one? Put me on wide speaker. I want to talk to him. What's his name?'

Al pressed the loudspeaker icon on screen and the phone beeped. 'Will, there's someone who wants to—'

'Ahoy! Ahoy!' Mursili shouted, making Will recoil. 'Will? Is that right? Mursili here. Did you ever do "water"? I was the librarian in Hattusa.'

Will still looked wary. 'Is that – Do I—'

Lexi stepped in. 'It's a phone. That's a phone in the 21st century. A telephone.'

'Seriously? This isn't some—' Will reached for the phone and took it from Al. He turned it over to check for wires and then took a close look at the screen. 'It's nothing like a telephone. Not one of the standard bits of the telephone's there.'

'You should try coming from 3,000 years ago,' Mursili's voice said. 'You must be from some time much closer if you have a phone.'

'1918. Do I just—' Will pointed to the phone. Al nodded.

'1918. So easy.' Al turned the volume down, but Mursili's voice was still pretty loud. 'If you meet oncoming oxen at a crossroads in 1918, do you have to sacrifice? No. If you build a new house, do you have to bury a goat's placenta beneath the corner posts or risk the wrath of the god Naamek? No. And Naamek's no pushover. Always wanting more placenta.'

Lexi tried to explain it. 'We brought Mursili here—'

Mursili cut in again. 'And now I'm on the team, Will. I'll help you adjust. I'm team librarian. When "okay" went off, Al and Lexi called me and I looked it up for them. You had movies in 1918? I'm like that guy in the control room with all the screens who goes in and shoots all his scenes in one day.'

'Mursili, we'll—'

'We'll have to meet.' Mursili was already onto his next idea. 'You might have knowledge that'll let us fine-tune what we do.'

'Good. Tomorrow, Mursili,' Al said clearly. 'Tomorrow. We'll sort out a time in the morning.'

'Good. Very good. Tomorrow. Ahoy, then.' With that he was gone.

'The guy in the control room with the screens—' Will looked baffled.

'Sorry,' Lexi said. 'That was a bit too much 21st century at once, wasn't it? Mursili still hasn't worked the phone out. He's from 1180BC. He doesn't realise you have to leave spaces, take turns, things like that. And he and Al are trying to bring back "ahoy" for answering the phone, which is a bit embarrassing.'

'Ah, Alexander Graham Bell.' Finally something sort of made sense. 'Really?'

'Just for "hello",' Al said, as if that made it all right. 'I don't do it for "goodbye" or anything. That was all him.' Lexi and Will were both laughing. 'It didn't feel so nerdy till right now.'

They took leftover sausages to Will once dinner had finished. It wouldn't have worked to turn up with a 19-year-old guy as their new friend and expect their parents to feed him.

He slept in the ferns that night. It was summer and no one ever went down that side of the house. He said he'd done far worse over the past four years.

The following day was Sunday, and Lexi and Al insisted to their parents that they'd been planning all week to meet friends for a movie at the El Dorado. Lexi even showed where it was on the calendar in the kitchen. She had written it there the night before. Their mother offered to drive them, but they said that'd be embarrassing, since everyone else was catching the bus.

Al hated catching the bus. He knew his mother would bring up the conversation any time he wanted a lift in future. 'But wouldn't it embarrass you?' she'd say. 'Wouldn't you be much happier on the bus?' It would work for now, though.

They met Will at the bus stop, as planned. They caught the bus to somewhere near the cinema, since that would look right if they were seen, but when they got there they

went to an ATM instead and got him some cash. It was odd watching their world through his eyes – all the traffic moving so quickly, and people wearing so little and carrying tiny machines that played music, sent messages, took photos and sometimes also happened to be phones. He couldn't tell the devices apart.

'The iPod Shuffle's much smaller.' Lexi pointed one out on a woman who was walking past. 'Too small to be a phone. You need a keyboard, or at least keys on a screen.'

'What about the guy with the piece of black plastic hooked on his ear?' Will could see a man in a suit standing at a cab rank by himself and talking.

'That's a phone, too, or part of one.'

'No, seriously. I know I'm new here, but I'm not going to believe everything's a phone.' He leant in close to the badge on her top. 'Hello, hello. Is this a phone?'

Lexi laughed and pushed him away. 'It's got Bluetooth, the phone that guy's using.'

'Bluetooth? Harald Gormsson?'

Now it was Lexi's turn not to get it. 'How do you know his name? You only got here yesterday.'

'Not him. Not the guy on the phone. Harald the king of Norway and Denmark in the 10th century. Son of Gorm the Old. The word "hustings" takes you there. Something does. They called him Bluetooth.'

Al took his phone from his pocket and jumped online. 'Watch this.' He went to Wikipedia and entered 'Bluetooth'. He scrolled down to the section headed 'Name and logo'.

'It's him.' He turned the screen towards Will. 'The phone company named it after him.'

He wondered if the word would last. Maybe it would. And maybe one day it'd go off and a word hunter from the future would find themselves in the meeting at Ericsson in 1994 when names were debated and Bluetooth came out on top. Al pictured it like the newspaper boardroom in Chicago in "okay", but with Ikea furniture and no smoking. Then the peg would lock into the portal, a thousand years would be gone in seconds, King Harald would appear. There would be a war on, more than likely.

Will read the Wikipedia entry and then took the phone and checked it front and back. 'How was that in there? How did you know to have it on the screen?'

What he needed was an explanation of the past century, and Lexi and Al made a start on it. Al tried to imagine stepping into a movie about the future. That was what Will was doing right now.

But he talked like them. Will looked and mostly sounded 21st century. At school in the lead-up to Anzac Day they had read letters from World War I soldiers, and the way they put things was different. There were hints of that when Will spoke, but not many.

'It's like you're still carrying a peg,' Al said, though he knew Will's pegs had gone in the 19th century.

Will reached down the neck of his T-shirt and pulled out a string. On the end of it he had peg keys – dozens of them. He had threaded them on and kept them with him.

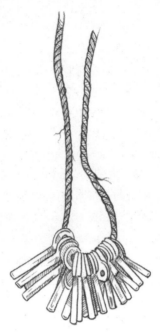

'The keys break off in the lock sometimes.' He slipped
them back into his shirt. 'I don't know if you've noticed that.
It's good to have a few spares. Maybe enough keys together
work a bit like a peg, as far as speaking and understanding
goes.' He shrugged. 'There's a lot of this word-hunter lark
that's not easy to work out. I am only from last century,
though – not 3,000 years ago.'

Mursili called out to them from across the street. He
stepped right into the traffic and a car braked hard and hit
its horn. He waved to the driver and patted the bonnet as he
walked in front of it, as if it was the head of a horse. Then,
before making it to the kerb, he nearly collided with a cyclist
coming the other way.

'Goodness, I'm amazed so many of you live to be adults,' he said.

'We cross at the lights.' Lexi pointed towards the intersection. 'And there's this whole stopping and looking right and left thing that we'll have to teach you.'

'I'm glad to hear you still do that.' Will stood up and held out his hand to Mursili. 'An early 20th-century invention that's still useful – how to cross the road. I'm Will.'

'"Where there's a Will there's a way" – I just learnt that one. It's a saying these people have.' Mursili shook Will's hand as if he was pumping water. 'Mursili. Formerly supreme librarian to the royal court of Suppiluliuma II and the Empire of Hatti. Currently deputy librarian, Cubberla Creek State School. But we have the internet now. It's not a come-down. Not at all.'

Mursili had already been thinking about what Will would need, and said he thought he could get him a tax file number. The more they all talked about life in the 21st century – drivers' licences and ID points for bank accounts and PINs and passwords – the more unnecessarily complicated Will thought the world had become.

He decided he would be a gardener for now, until the tax file number came through. That way he could work for cash. Al was pretty sure that wasn't legal, but since Will technically didn't exist in the 21st century, it was probably safe enough.

'I'll design flyers for you,' Lexi said. 'I can make them look great. But you'll need a point of contact.'

'Easy.' Lexi had jumped in with the offer of flyers and Al didn't want to be left behind. 'Mum and Dad have a fleet plan, and they never use it all. We could probably get you one of their old phones.'

'Your parents have a fleet?' Yet again, the new century was keeping Will off-balance. 'A fleet of what?'

'We all have phones on the one plan.' As soon as he said it, Al realised it made no sense in 1918. 'The family's got a bunch of phones, but they're all covered by one monthly bill. I'm sure it'll be okay.'

'Do people say "okay" much?' It had been on Will's mind for a while. 'We didn't in England in 1918, but you did just then. I didn't know if it was going to last. Through disuse, I mean, not through it having four steps.'

'Five steps,' Lexi said. 'If you mean the different time periods we had to go to when we hunted it. You wouldn't have seen 1929, with the "O-K-A-Y" spelling. Just "O" and "K" still works, though.' She couldn't imagine life without 'OK'. It was everywhere. She was forever pressing 'OK' or clicking on it.

'It's even more brittle with that extra step. You don't get many words with five.'

'What do you mean?' Al was thinking it too, but Lexi asked it. 'What do you mean "brittle"?'

'Well, the more steps, the more at risk it is.' Will shrugged, as if it was obvious. But Lexi and Al were looking at him blankly. 'Have you noticed how, in a language with thousands of words, some of them get triggered a lot more often than others? No one knows all the reasons for that, but one factor is how many steps a word has to go through to exist in the present. The more steps, the more often it'll break down. Plenty of words have one or two steps, so they're more stable.'

'But "okay"?' Lexi couldn't imagine losing it, or it unexisting. 'If you think about it, it's probably the most widely used word in the world. It could be the first word to go into practically every language. Dad said when he was in China with work, credit card machines still had an "OK" button on them and he heard people on the phone speaking Chinese and saying "okay".'

Will groaned and Mursili stepped in. 'Not making sense? Credit card machines? A credit card is a plastic rectangle with a magnetised strip to store information about your money. It lets you spend money when you don't have cash. Sometimes your own money from your bank account, but often it's money that you don't have and that you're borrowing.'

'Oh, like "broke"?' Will looked at Lexi and Al. 'Have you done "broke"? Borrowers' tiles?' They hadn't. 'Eighteenth-century Italy, banks handing out borrowers' tiles with the customer's name and credit limit on them. If the customer went over the limit, the bank broke the tile.'

They compared words they'd hunted. Will had done more than 40 during his nine months with the dictionary. He could practically recite them all. He'd had four lost years to think about them, in case any one of them offered a way out of the 1830s.

'What about the Battle of Hastings?' Lexi wanted their four missions to count for something too, even if he'd been on far more. 'If you haven't done "water", did anything else take you to the Battle of Hastings?'

'Hastings was just one day, wasn't it?' He said it as if it couldn't have been a big deal. 'My toughest battle was against the Aztecs. They mightn't have had guns, but there were thousands of them and they never stopped coming at you. That was "cocoa". First I thought it wasn't up to much, since it mainly seemed to be about Doctor Johnson making a mistake in his dictionary, but suddenly you're waging war outside Tenochtitlan. It's hot and everyone's got diarrhoea and 50,000 men want to sacrifice you alive in the hope that it'll change their luck. Now *that's* a battle.'

'Hastings was a totally serious battle.' Al tried not to sound annoyed. 'It was a massacre. Pretty much the whole English army dies, and you're in it. Eight thousand men. Maybe ten. All on one hillside.'

Will nodded. 'Sorry. I didn't mean to insult you. I don't think any battle's easy. It's always nice to get a word that doesn't have one. And there are plenty. Lots of words come from plays and printing errors. And unreasonable things people said in the 17th century about the Dutch.'

It was a relief to hear that. Lexi wanted more of those words. As she saw people crossing the street at the lights on their way to the El Dorado for a movie, she wanted that life back. She wanted Sundays to be simple and safe, and to have hours that weren't spent working through past battles or their next move into the past.

Among the group bunching up to cross the road, she noticed a girl in an orange hat. Not a towelling hat like her grandfather's in the photos, but it was enough. She thought of Grandad Al and the fish, Grandad Al on sports day, Grandad Al lost and with all kinds of mean and strange theories about it, and only she and Al could save him.

She hadn't fought Montezuma, but she had fought. She knew what it felt like when cavalry charged, when archers filled the sky with arrows, when a mace bit into your flesh. She wouldn't ever be the same again. She couldn't forget it. She watched the moviegoers on this summer Sunday and knew she could go, but she couldn't be one of them anymore. And she didn't want to be.

There were only three people in the world who understood her. One was a librarian over 3,000 years old, another was a skater dude closing in on a 110, and the third was her irritating but essential brother. A month ago she'd been cool, and staying cool had been all she'd needed to worry about. Life wasn't like that now.

'There's one more thing,' Will said when they were almost back at the bus stop. 'I really want to ask Caractacus this one. Have you noticed that, sometimes, if you go back more than a few hundred years, it's as if someone's watching you, maybe even hunting you?'

Al started to say no, but Lexi interrupted him. 'Teutoburg Forest. We'd almost got away from the battle when these two guys came out of nowhere. It really seemed like they were out to get us. And they didn't look like the Romans or the local people.'

Will nodded. 'Were they wearing grey robes?'

'Yes.' She stopped walking. 'How did you know that?'

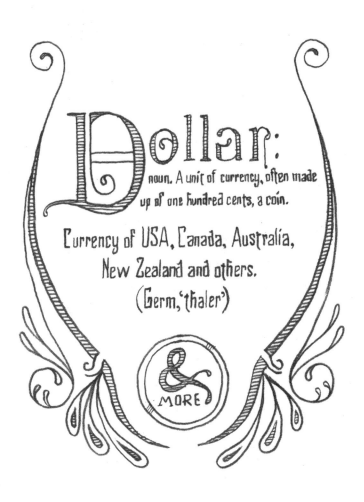

# Dollar:

noun. A unit of currency, often made up of one hundred cents, a coin.

Currency of USA, Canada, Australia, New Zealand and others.
(Germ. "thaler")

& MORE

ILL WAS STAYING in a dorm room at a youth hostel when the next word mission came through. It was the kind of place his family would have completely freaked out about in 1918, and he was loving it. Everyone seemed to get on with each other and, any time he was near the pool, German and Scandinavian female backpackers seemed to need him to rub sunscreen on their backs.

He kept promising the manager that he would find his ID to register properly, but Mursili was still working on that. Will could get an express copy of his birth certificate from London within days, but it'd take a credit card he didn't have and it'd say 1903, which wouldn't help his case.

He told the manager he'd been robbed once when he was sleeping in a park, and he'd lost everything. He didn't say it had happened in the northern summer of 1836.

Music had come a long way since 1918, and was now played all night and loud. From the music videos in the bar in the hostel basement, it seemed that all black American people were now rich and highly desirable. He wanted to tell the backpackers how great this was – so much better than in the early 19th century and even the 20th – but he thought they wouldn't get it. They hardly seemed to see colour at all. Everyone danced with everyone. If it was all like this, he

totally loved the 21st century, even if he still missed home.

Then he got the text from Lexi saying that the dictionary had gone off again and the word was 'dollar'.

He texted back, 'Not one I've done. C U soon.' He finished his coffee and checked that he had his Go Card in his pocket. If the buses worked out right, he could just make it back to the hostel before the end of dollar pizza – it was three dollars a slice after six. His backpack was ready in his room.

Mursili was with Lexi and Al in the park when he arrived. Al was holding the dictionary.

'It went off when we were at school.' He showed Will the open page. 'I don't know how long it's been going for.'

'We've got a while.' Will took the dictionary and read the definition. 'They last for a while.'

'I've looked it up,' Mursili said. 'It should take you back no more than 500 years. That'll be in Europe. German-speaking Europe. I can't say for sure where you'll go between now and then. It should be relatively battle-free, though.'

For a moment no one spoke. They watched the '& more' button blinking and braced themselves for the fall and whatever might follow it.

'I'll step back, then,' Mursili said. 'See you in a minute.'

Will turned the dictionary Lexi's way. 'Ladies first. As we said in 1918.'

She blushed and reached for the button.

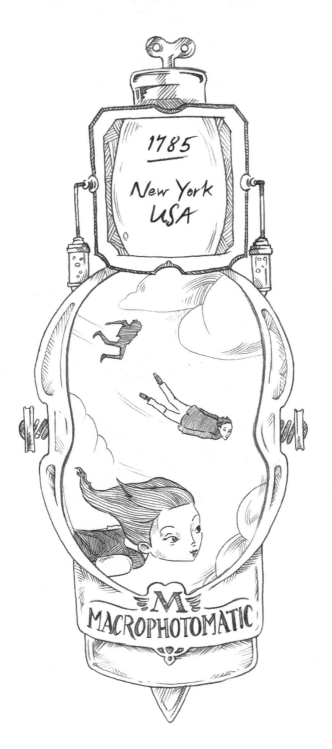

$\mathcal{T}$HEY SHUDDERED OVER the grammar-manual bumps of the past century and a half and then veered sideways. Lexi noticed that, while Al still tumbled and she did her best not to, Will flew easily and the wind blew his hair back as he fell. She'd seen a picture of a girl called Dagmar on his phone, and wondered if Dagmar was his girlfriend.

As the air cleared, she hadn't expected to see New York again quite so soon. But it wasn't 19th century New York or the New York of Hudson's *Half Moon* voyage. It was somewhere in-between: a town on the southern part of Manhattan. There were fields and empty blocks and damaged buildings. And a crowd.

Will angled his flight to steer clear of the people on the street and the others followed. They landed at the next corner.

The crowd had gathered around an impressive stone building with columns at the front and a red roof.

'Oh, great. Buckles.' Al took a look at his shoes. 'At least Will and I've both got them. And are these leggings or—'

'Breeches, I think.' Will had a mustard-coloured suit, with a thigh-length waistcoat and breeches ending at white stockings from the knee down. He wasn't going to mock anyone for what they were wearing.

'And yet again I'm not supposed to move.' Lexi's dress had fitted sleeves and a narrow waist, but puffed out below there in numerous petticoats. Her backpack was now a wicker basket, while Al and Will had matching black satchels over their shoulders. 'I can't believe I've got to carry all this in my hand.'

They had left the 21st century with loaded backpacks. That had been Will's idea. They had ropes, muesli bars, whistles, matches – the list went on, and was an updated version of what Will had learnt to pack in 1918. Each of them also had a photo of Grandad Al. The key badges might help any lost word hunter find them, but this way they could also ask if people had seen him.

The one thing they'd ruled out taking was weapons. Will had tried it with hunting knives and an air pistol and they had all vanished. So Lexi and Al's knife going missing hadn't been a one-off. Will had his own list of questions for Caractacus and the missing weapons were on it.

Al checked the pegs. 'Four this time.' He showed the others the one that had activated.

Doug blinked up at the rectangle of daylight. He smelt stale sweat, perfume, occasional horse poo. And someone was roasting nuts.

'The War of Independence is over, then.' Will looked down the street into the distance. 'Two years ago. Do you think it's what wrecked those buildings? There's been a fire. The one at the end of the street looks like it was a church.' He focused his attention on the crowd and the building across the road. A banner hung from the balcony and it read 'Congress of the Confederation'. 'That looks like the spot for us. "Dollar." What's it going to be?'

Al had expected a team decision, but Will was already on his way. Just because the building was the obvious place to start didn't mean it was right. History didn't always happen in big buildings. But he had to catch Will to tell him that, and Will had already made his move. He and Lexi were checking the pillars below the balcony for word-hunter initials when Al reached them.

'Come in, come in,' an usher said. 'We have only a few more seats.' He directed them towards the door. 'They're debating currency.'

Al kept his complaint to himself. He would have picked the building too, after a quick look around.

At least 'dollar' looked easy so far. They took their seats in the back row. At the front of the chamber, the representatives were sitting on wooden seats arranged in rows on a platform. They all sat side-on to the audience. Some rows of seats were on the left of the temporary stage, some on the right, and all the representatives faced the middle. One man sat on a raised chair against the back wall.

He tapped something against the arm of the chair and the crowd went quiet, waiting for him to speak.

He nodded to acknowledge their silence. 'Our final speaker before a short recess shall be the United States Minister to France and former congressman for Virginia, Mr Thomas Jefferson, happily back among us for this sitting.'

Thomas Jefferson stood up. 'Thank you, Mr Speaker.' His hair was starting to grey and it curled under at the ends. He cleared his throat and checked his notes. 'My views shall come

as no surprise to those who know me.' Some of the others were nodding as if they were on his side already. 'For those who do not, I refer to my written proposal of 1782. The matter of our currency is one of both practical and symbolic importance. We are independent from Britain, and should demonstrate that at every opportunity. There are still pounds in circulation in our country, but so is the Spanish eight-real piece, which we have come to know as the Spanish dollar, and so is the Maria Theresa thaler of our friends in Continental Europe.'

At the mention of the Spanish dollar, Lexi, Al and Will all looked around, but there was no sign of a portal yet. Al straightened his breeches and sat back in the wooden chair.

He told himself it was good there were three of them now. He and Lexi no longer had to make every decision themselves, find every portal themselves, fight every battle without a clue about how to do it. Will might have ideas about being in charge, but Al felt less responsible and, if he was honest, less scared. That counted for something. Will had experience and looked fit and in control. When they had first met him in the coach house in Plymouth he looked hungry and almost frightened. Perhaps he'd been afraid of being wrong, getting his hopes up and then staying stuck in 1839.

Thomas Jefferson was holding paper money in one hand. 'I know that some would favour "Continental" as the name, and the Continental served us well in time of war. But the future is not its time. Inflation has rendered it worthless, and these Continentals I hold are printed in three different currencies, including the British pound. We cannot use the British pound, even on our own notes. I therefore propose that the unit of currency of these United States be, across the nation, called the dollar. The dollar is a known coin, and the most familiar of all to the mind of the people. It is already adopted from south to north. It is the recommendation of Mr Howell's grand committee. I have a proposer and a seconder.' He nodded towards two of the seated men. 'And I ask you, after this recess, to give their resolution your full support.'

There was applause from the congressmen before he sat down, and the audience joined in, first simply because applause had started and then because they knew what it meant. It was a further step towards independence, another block on which to build a nation, and that was something to celebrate.

The woman next to Al stood, still applauding, and the basket on her arm bumped Al's elbow. There was a loaf of bread sticking out of it, with a chunk missing at the end. Doug was poking out of Al's coat pocket, gnawing away at it. Al shook his coat and Doug fell back down out of sight. Even when history was being made, a rat would ignore it if there was bread on offer.

The Speaker called for order and asked for the wording of the resolution to be circulated during the recess.

The congressmen stood and the crowd followed. Suddenly everyone was talking at once.

'I'll get to where they're sitting and check for a portal,' Will said. 'You two get your pictures out.'

For the next half-hour they made their way through the audience and most of the congressmen, but no one knew Grandad Al. Quite a few commented on the quality of the image, and Lexi and Al put it down to a new engraving technique. No one noticed their key badges. By the time the Speaker called the house to order again, they were sure there were no word hunters there.

If they could find the portal, they could leave with it and search the streets, travel even further. But they had no leads. This wasn't Nantucket. America went on and on beyond the Hudson River and 1785 was only one year in the long history of English. They would search systematically each time, but then they would go. That was the deal.

'Nothing,' Will said as they sat down again. 'If it's gone off I couldn't find it. Not even any initials, but I put some on a column down at the front.'

No Grandad Al, no lost word hunters, no portal. Not yet.

'The resolution proposed by the congressmen is a simple one,' the Speaker said. He had a single sheet of paper in his hand. 'That the money unit of the United States of America be one dollar. All in favour please say "aye".' All the congressmen seemed to say it, loudly and clearly. One banged his walking stick against the floor. 'All against, please say "nay".' There was silence. 'Let it be recorded that it was passed on the voices that the money unit of the United States of America be one dollar.'

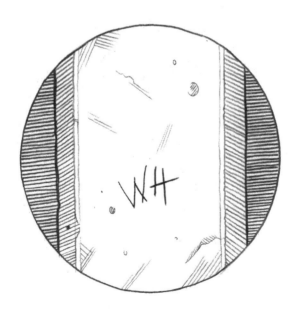

Applause broke out again, this time beginning in the audience and spreading to the stage. The Speaker made no move to stop it. It was history being made and a roomful of people who knew it. It was times like this that Al most wanted to tell people about – America could have gone for the Continental or something else, but the dollar was chosen in a particular place and at a particular moment and he had been there to see it.

The Speaker made a note on the copy of the resolution in his hand, and passed it to a clerk. It was then that it started to glow.

The word hunters left their seats as the clerk stepped from the platform and made his way down the side of the chamber towards a table with documents on it.

'You two distract him,' Will said. 'I'll get behind him and take the resolution.'

It felt as though Will was doing the hard part of the job, until Al realised there was no plan for distracting the clerk. He thought back through Thomas Jefferson's speech.

'Got it,' he said. 'Leave it to me, Lex.'

They reached the clerk as he was setting the resolution on the table. Will looked ahead into the crowd, pretended to see someone he knew and waved. He took a step past the clerk.

'Excuse me, sir,' Al said. 'I have a question.'

'Of course you do.' The clerk sounded less than interested. 'Everyone has a question at these open sessions. That's the idea.'

'If the Spanish call their eight-real piece eight reales, why do we call it the Spanish dollar?'

The man rolled his eyes as if Al was clueless. 'Why? Because it's not Dutch.'

Will had the resolution in his hand and he ducked behind a column. Al thanked the clerk – though he didn't know what he had to thank him for – and waved at the same spot in the crowd as Will had. The clerk muttered something about open sessions, checked his table and wondered where he'd put the resolution.

As the others reached him, Will touched the '& more' button glowing from the 'o' of the word 'dollar'.

'Why can't it always be this easy?' he said, as Al drove the peg into the portal.

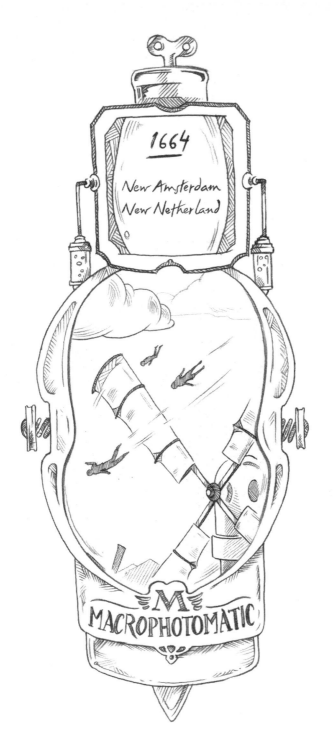

THEY DROPPED STRAIGHT down, quickly at first and then more slowly. As the air cleared and the pressure left his chest, Al started to wonder just how English the English language was. They were falling towards Manhattan for the fifth time in just one-and-a-half words.

This time, most of the island was forest or grassland or farms, but the bottom tip had a wall across it, marking the edge of a town. So it was after Hudson, after 1609. There were streets of white houses with canals cut between them, a windmill and a star-shaped fortress. The gardens had trees in neat rows and paths marking the lawns and beds into diamonds.

There were ships docked in the harbour and four more approaching from the sea, sailing together. A crowd was gathering on the docks and the word hunters angled into a glide that would drop them nearby.

Will was the first to steady himself on his feet. 'They're all going to be Dutch, aren't they?' He glanced at the crowd and then checked his own clothes. He had a big black hat with a buckle on it that matched the buckles on his shoes. His black coat reached most of the way to the ground, or at least all the way to his pale blue knee-high stockings. 'This is going to be New Amsterdam.'

'Eight reales was the Spanish dollar because it wasn't Dutch.' Al was beginning to think the clerk's comment mightn't be irrelevant after all. 'Are there Dutch dollars here? Is this when they arrive or—'

'Yeah, great,' Lexi said. 'Any chance we could stop loving the history for a second and take a look at the peg?'

'Only once we've finished talking about your hat.' This time Al was dressed like a pirate, while Lexi wore a lacy version of the hairnets worn by the deli staff in Coles, a lacy collar and more than likely several petticoats.

She folded her arms and scowled at him. 'We've got two more steps after this one. You're going to score some leggings before we're home.'

The peg confirmed their guess about the place and the people, but neither Will nor Al could pin anything specific down to 1664. Something was about to happen, though. Everyone in the crowd was looking out to sea at the four ships coming in.

Almost everyone. Not far from where the word hunters had landed an argument was going on. One man was ramming a stick down the barrel of a cannon that was pointing at the ships and two others were trying to stop him.

'There's no point, Petrus,' an older man in a black coat like Will's said to the man standing next to him. 'It will only do more harm.'

The crew on the gun was waiting for orders from Petrus. He had long black hair, a huge white collar and a wooden right leg with ornamental silverwork. People were clustered around him, waiting for his decision.

'I know that,' he said. 'And you know how many petitions I've sent to head office, demanding soldiers and more cannon. They chose to build a fort and put almost nothing in it. We're lucky this took so long to happen.' He turned to the cannon crew, specifically to the man with a burning torch. 'Hold your fire.'

'Hey, it's literal,' Al said, more to himself than anyone else. '"Hold your fire." As in, hold on to your torch and don't light the—'

'Focus.' Lexi elbowed him in the arm. 'I know the past can be chock-full of history sometimes, but maybe save it for later?'

With the aid of his cane, Petrus walked over to the edge of the dock, where he was helped to stand on a wooden trunk. From there he could see everyone who had gathered around – all the colonists and traders and local Lenape trappers who had come with beaver pelts. There was timber piled on the dock and there were bales of dried tobacco leaf from the West Indies.

'Be proud of what you've done,' Petrus said. 'You are people with differences, who have lived and traded peacefully. Some of you would fight today; many of you would seek a peace. A negotiated peace is our only option. Each of the British ships has twice the cannon of our colony and each has at least 100 men aboard. We are not an army. I will not see lives wasted. We will stand back from our cannon, look stronger than we are and make the best peace we can.'

The cannon crew moved back, and ground the burning torch out on the stones of the dock. The British took this as the signal it was, and moved closer.

'Looks like the end of the Dutch dollar, then,' Will said. 'The British'll want any money that's here, but the Dutch'll want to keep it. Either way the currency'll change. At least officially. They'll talk about money when they negotiate. Which means sticking close to the man with the fancy leg. He'll be the one handling the Dutch end of it.'

As the British ships closed in, the crews stood at their cannons, ready for any sign of attack. Ropes were thrown from both ends of the first ship and the Dutch secured it to

the dock. A wide plank was pushed from the deck until it
reached the stone wharf.

The tension in the crowd rose as two unarmed British
officers stepped ashore, along with a man who had high curly
hair, a long deep-red leather coat and a scarf.

'Director-General Stuyvesant,' he said to Petrus,
having recognised him by the silver on his leg, 'I am Richard
Nicolls, come with a commission from His Royal Highness
the Duke of York to take control of territories granted to him
by the King of England, and which are currently called, by
your company, New Netherland.'

He took a document from a pocket in his coat and
opened it. Even from a distance, a large red wax seal could be

seen at the bottom. He offered it to Petrus Stuyvesant, who didn't move.

'Mr Nicolls,' he said. 'Your ships are welcome to dock while we discuss this. I would ask that your men come ashore only to buy provisions, should your crews require them. Our troops shall also remain in their quarters. I will have three of my own horses brought to take your delegation to my farm.'

'Sir,' Richard Nicolls said, loud enough for everyone to hear it, 'I am commissioned to make a peace that promises life, estate and liberty to all who would submit to the king's authority.'

Some people in the crowd nodded. It was what they'd hoped to hear.

'We will do this peacefully, then,' Petrus Stuyvesant said, 'if by liberty you include the liberty to worship in the way we see fit and not exactly as your king does.' He paused and this time the crowd cheered. 'And if by estate you mean that every person here can keep their house, lands, goods and every daalder in their possession, and be subjected to no future unfair taxes.'

Another cheer rose and a glow came from one of Petrus Stuyvesant's pockets. Al saw it first and pointed it out to the others.

'It's money,' Lexi said. 'The daalder is the Dutch dollar. It's a coin in his pocket – a daalder in his possession.'

'This one doesn't look so easy.' Al couldn't see Petrus Stuyvesant taking his coat off anywhere between here and his farm.

'You've never picked a pocket before?' Will was smiling. 'I just have to get close enough.'

Lexi wasn't sure they'd ever know all of Will's past. Maybe it was better that way. Maybe being a word hunter changed you, but there were things she didn't want to change. She'd stolen food, but that was because she needed to eat. They'd taken things from a library, but the library was burning down. And now the new portal was a dollar in someone's pocket. His dollar, but their portal.

The chance to take it came when the horses arrived. There were two for the British officers, one for Richard Nicolls and Petrus Stuyvesant's own favourite horse. One handler looked after all of them, while the terms for the meeting were discussed. The horses looked skittish, with the street full of people and the noise of rumours and defiance and fear. Businesses were closing as quickly as they could, the owners dragging their wares inside and bolting their doors.

'This is it,' Will said. 'You two skirt around the horses and, as soon as you're past them, give a loud blast on your whistles. Then duck into the crowd and make your way back.'

'That's not a whole plan.' Al wanted to have his say. 'What are we whistling for? How is that going to—'

'I'll have the daalder by the time Stuyvesant's on his horse. That's the plan. You're the distraction, and I get the coin. He won't even know.' Will could see that Petrus Stuyvesant and the Englishmen were ready to leave. 'We have to move right now or we miss our chance.'

'Let's go.' Lexi took Al by the arm and turned him away from Will. 'Get your whistle out.'

Al had no better plan and there was no time to argue. He swung his duffel bag down from his shoulder and reached into it for his whistle.

With Lexi, he made his way through the crowd, keeping the horses in the corner of his vision and making every move look as though it was about something else. He hoped Will was good at picking pockets. If he got caught ...

It was better not to think about that. He felt the whistle pressing into the palm of his closed hand. Lexi was keeping her eyes down, but she glanced his way as they passed the horses. She nodded. They brought their hands to their mouths.

The noise of the two whistles was shrill and piercing – way louder than when they'd tested them in the park at home. An old man next to them dropped his walking stick and fell to his knees. A woman spilt bread from her basket. Three of the four horses panicked and one stood still.

And Doug shrieked as if the end of the world had come, burst from the top of Al's duffel bag and leapt into the crowd.

'Doug!' Al turned, but Lexi grabbed his arm.

'He'll find us. Hide your whistle.' She pulled him back into the crowd.

Doug scrambled across the cobbles, dodging around people's feet. The whistles were still screeching in his head.

Ahead of him, the handler almost had the horses back under control when Doug burst from the crowd and ran up

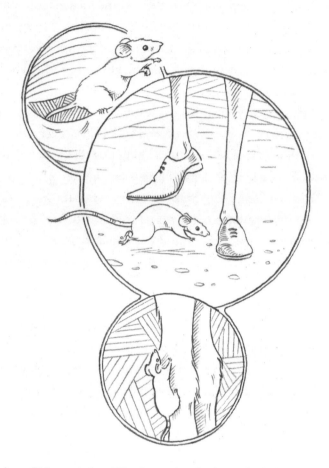

the still horse's leg. The horse bucked, yanked the handler's arm and set the other three off again.

'Let me help.' Will stepped forward and grabbed at the reins, making sure he took the two biggest, fittest horses. Petrus Stuyvesant wouldn't be letting the British ride higher in the saddle.

The handler wrapped the reins of the other two around the wrist of his good arm and let his injured arm fall by his side. 'I think he's dislocated my shoulder.' His face was scrunched up with pain. 'He's deaf, this one. Don't know what set him off.'

Will spoke to the two horses to calm them. They were still fidgety, so he took both sets of reins in one hand, swung his duffel bag from his shoulder and dug around in it until he found a muesli bar. He held pieces of it out on his flat palm, and the horses ate them and settled.

Petrus Stuyvesant gave Richard Nicolls the second biggest horse and turned to Will to help him onto the biggest. Will took his cane and, as the director-general swung his wooden leg over the horse, Will's hand seemed to touch his coat to steady him.

Even though she was watching closely, Lexi saw nothing.

Al was kneeling, clicking his fingers, searching the world at rat height, peering among all the pale stockings and bulky dresses in the hope of seeing Doug.

Will patted the flank of the horse, Petrus Stuyvesant flicked the reins and the horse moved forward, leading the other three behind it. The crowd watched as the negotiators rode past the fortress and up Broadway, towards the director-general's farm.

'They're getting away,' Al said as Will came over to them. 'And I can't find Doug. I can't find him anywhere. I don't know where—'

'Don't worry.' Will opened a pocket in his coat and Doug poked his head out. 'Who do you think scared the deaf horse? It might have been a lot harder without this little fellow. In the end, it wasn't hard at all.'

He opened another pocket and the golden glow from the coin lit up his hand.

'How did you—' Lexi leant over to take a closer look.

'I'll teach you, if you really want to know.' He swung his duffel bag down and got out his picture of Grandad Al. 'All right. Let's check this crowd.'

Al took Doug in his hand and opened his own bag. As he reached in for the picture, he touched something moist and pellety.

He groaned. 'Rat poo. I just touched poo!' Doug looked at him and blinked. 'I know the whistle scared you, but did you have to?'

Will laughed at him. 'It's the 17th century. People touch poo all the time. Toughen up. And get your photo out while we've still got a crowd to show it to.'

Al lifted the coiled rope from his bag and tipped the poo onto the cobblestones. He hoped he'd got all of it. He scraped his hand across the cobbles in case there was still poo on it. In the future they would bring wet wipes, since that was what 21st-century non-poo-touching people did.

They got nowhere with the picture. No one could place Grandad Al. No one noticed their key badges.

'No initials, either,' Will said when they got together again at the end of the dock, close to where they'd arrived. 'Maybe we're the first here.'

He crouched down, wrote 'WH' in pencil on a pale stone and left a rubber band beside it.

Across the water, beyond the trading ships and the ships of the British navy, Lexi could see the mainland. She swapped her basket from her right hand to her left. It was getting heavy. The dictionary included thousands of words, each with a past. Any one of them might hold Grandad Al. And all the rest might send them into danger on the edge of wild country, hundreds of years before their own time.

'He's not here,' Will said. 'We can tick this one off. Let's try the next one.'

He took the daalder from his pocket, rubbed it with his thumb and the portal opened up.

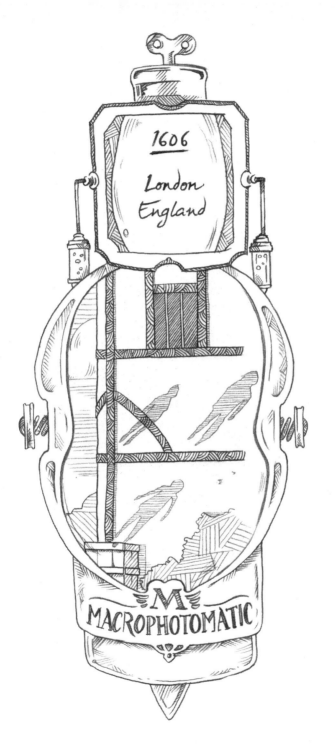

*T*HEY FELL AT a comfortable speed before hitting a bump as they left cloud. Al felt the dense air punch into his chest. And then stop punching, as if it had never started. As if there had been no bump at all.

He remembered a bump below Doctor Johnson's dictionary on Caractacus's timeline. It was Shakespeare. They were falling exactly into the middle of the Shakespeare bump, falling towards a wide, grey crowded city that could only be London.

'This way,' Will said and he banked to lead them south of the river, towards a large thatched letter 'O'.

They dropped through the centre of it, clear of the rectangular roof that jutted in from the edge, and slowed to a soft landing on ground covered by straw, nutshells and bottle stoppers. They were in a stadium or an arena, with wide timber posts holding up three levels of seating. There was room for thousands of people, though no one was there at the moment. No one other than the men on stage.

'William Shakespeare,' Will whispered, pointing to one with a high forehead and a neat moustache and beard. 'I'm called Will after him. This is the Globe Theatre. My parents were introduced at *Romeo and Juliet* in the '90s. The 1890s. You'd have your own '90s, wouldn't you?'

'Well, not personally. We just missed the '90s. We'll try to catch them next time around.' Lexi wanted to say something smart about *Romeo and Juliet*. The Shakespeare connection seemed to mean a lot to Will. She and Al hadn't done Shakespeare yet.

Al opened his sack and started looking for the peg. He had crumpled yellow pants that went down to his calves and a rough brown coat with a rope belt.

Lexi laughed. 'You look like a weedy banana.' She and Will both had the same clothes as Al, but in off-white. Somehow she was suggesting that was better.

'And you look like you're going to a judo class.' He pulled out the peg.

Doug blinked at him. He smelt hazelnuts and spilt beer and people were talking about bananas. This place could be good.

'I told you,' Will said when he saw the peg. 'It's Shakespeare.'

Lexi looked towards the stage. 'Shouldn't we move before they see us?'

'They're actors.' Al watched one of them take a step forward, then make a mark on the floor with his toe. 'They won't see us. They'd only notice us if we could get them a bigger part.'

Shakespeare was holding some pages in one hand and a quill pen in the other. He wasn't looking happy. The actors were standing in their positions on the stage, but no one seemed to be acting.

'But I've read Holinshed's *Chronicles*,' one of them said, as if it made him the best informed. 'Holinshed says Banquo was in on the murder of King Duncan and that it happened by ambush on the way to Inverness.'

Shakespeare looked annoyed. 'I've read Holinshed too, Richard. You can't write a draft of "Macbeth" without reading Holinshed. Everyone's read Holinshed. The king's bath cleaner's mother's read Holinshed.'

The other actors laughed.

'I didn't know she was writing a "Macbeth",' Richard said, making the others laugh again.

'Yes, "The King's Bath Cleaner's Mother's Macbeth".' Shakespeare used his hands to suggest it was written on a banner above the stage. 'Starring Richard Burbage as the man who couldn't get past Holinshed.' He folded his pages. 'There's a key piece of information Holinshed didn't know. It turns out that the king believes he is descended from Banquo and, since he's our patron and pays the bills, I thought the clever thing to do might be to back one of the versions of the story that doesn't say his ancestor was a murderer.'

'Hope you enjoy the new play, Your Majesty,' one of the others said in a grovelling crawly voice, bending over in an exaggerated bow and tugging at the front of his hair. 'We owe it all to you and your ancestors. Thank you so much for your money and your murdering.'

Everyone except Richard laughed at that. Shakespeare tried not to, but couldn't hold it in. He held up his hand to make another point.

'It's also more dramatic and all the more foul if Macbeth has it done in his own castle.'

Richard nodded. 'Of course. I can see that. And I'm all for drama. The play's the thing.'

He looked down at his pages and found the line he was up to.

He was about to deliver it when one of the other actors raised a finger and said, 'Just a small point, William.'

'Oh, you too, Robert.' Shakespeare gave him a look that suggested points of any size might not be very welcome. 'A point small enough that it'll still let me finish this play within, say, the 17th century?'

Robert faked an apologetic look. 'I just thought I'd bring it up now, while we're on a break from the lines.'

'We're *not* on a break from the lines.' Shakespeare jabbed his quill at the pages in his hand. 'This is us *doing the lines.*'

'Oh, I thought since we were talking about Holinshed – which I haven't read yet, by the way – and the king being from murderers and all—' He stopped. 'Perhaps I should get to my small point.'

'Perhaps.' Shakespeare maintained his glare.

Down on the straw, Will turned to Lexi and Al. 'Isn't this great? I love coming here. This is my fifth time, I think. That's almost as many times as I've seen Caractacus. I've wanted to ask Shakespeare why he hasn't written about those days – Arthur and all that lot. It'd get right up Caractacus's nose.' He laughed. 'Have you seen Shakespeare? One of his plays, I mean. They're good, but this is a lot better, watching them get written.'

'You'll thank me for this later,' Robert was saying on stage – though, from Shakespeare's look, it didn't seem likely. 'Some people are sticklers for detail, and you know they'll make a fuss. In act I, scene 3—'

'It's not even the bit we're doing.' Every time Shakespeare spoke, his impatience seemed to crank up a notch. 'When we do lines, *we talk about the bit we're doing.*'

He said it slowly and forcefully, as if Robert's capacity to grasp it was likely to be limited. He turned to the table behind him and set down the scene they were working on. He had the rest of the play there, laid out scene by scene.

'Yes, but I thought we weren't doing lines. That's when I said I had the small point.' Robert held his thumb and finger close together, as if Shakespeare's back might see it.

'Actors—' Shakespeare didn't turn around. 'It would be easier to teach kittens how to morris dance. But, please, your small point—' He picked up the scene.

Robert shuffled through a few pages, then shuffled back again. 'Actually, it's act I, scene 2, the line "Till he disbursed at Saint Colme's Inch ten thousand sovereigns to our general use".'

Shakespeare flicked through act I, slipped scene 3 in and pulled scene 2 out. 'Yes?' He turned and shrugged.

'It's the King of Norway, William,' Robert said, 'so would it be better with foreign money? Marks, maybe?'

'Well done, Robert. You were right to identify that as a small point. I'd be interested to see what you would call a very small point.' He searched through the pages until he could see the line himself. '"Marks" doesn't scan. Do you have no sense of rhythm at all? Can't you feel that it needs two syllables?' He read the line again. 'Dollars? That's foreign. I think it's even Norwegian. Daler. Does "dollar" work for you?'

For the past few minutes the word hunters hadn't thought about their mission, but the mention of dollars and the glow from the page as Shakespeare made the alteration with his quill changed that.

'There it is,' Al whispered, though the others had seen it too. 'Can we get it and then look for Grandad Al?'

'Don't see why not.' Will stood up. 'As soon as he puts the page down. The others have all got copies, so it's not as if "Macbeth" will end up a page short. Just follow my lead. I worked out how to get on stage quickly a couple of visits ago.' As the word hunters moved forward, Will called out to the men on stage, 'Sorry to interrupt, but we've been sent to make repairs.'

'Repairs to what?' Richard Burbage didn't seem to like the idea. 'And sent by whom? You do realise we own this theatre?'

'We're Mr Street's men.' Will strode towards the steps to the stage as if he'd been on them dozens of times. 'There's a problem with one of the beams. We need to get it sorted out before there's an audience in here.'

'All right, then.' Richard folded his pages. 'If Street thinks there's a problem, then there's a problem. Do you need us to move?'

'We should be able to work around you,' Will told him. 'We're just measuring for now. You can leave things where they are and keep ignoring us.'

Shakespeare checked the new wording of the line, tucked the scene back into act I and set it down on the table.

The actors had started reading again before the word hunters reached the steps.

As they crossed the back of the stage, it all seemed easy. There were no horses this time, or pockets to pick, or battles to fight. Now they were this close it was impossible not to watch the actors and Shakespeare, and 'Macbeth' taking shape. Al wanted to stop and tell them how famous it would be 400 years later, and that it looked set to be famous forever, this thing they were making here and now. He'd never seen the play, but he knew that.

As Will reached for act I, scene 2, a hand grabbed his wrist. There had been no one there seconds before.

'My friend,' the man who had grabbed him said. He had a cape, a tall dark hat and strange dark glasses, a black moustache and goatee. 'John Johnson. A moment—'

'Mr Street wants us to—' Will had barely got the words out when the man's other hand drew a knife from inside his cape.

Will jumped back, but John Johnson held on. Four men in grey robes ran from behind pillars and across the stage towards them. Will smashed John Johnson's arm onto the edge of the table and broke his grip. As the men in grey closed in, they pulled knives from their robes. One of them moved behind Will.

'Lexi, the table!' Al shouted.

They grabbed it by the legs and lifted it, scattering the carefully ordered scenes. They swung it hard and hit the man in the back, knocking him to the ground. His dagger clattered

to the floor, almost at Will's feet. As the man lunged forward to pick it up, Will kicked at it. It skidded across the stage and dropped off the edge into the straw.

Al felt someone pull at his sack and heard the clank of pegs and then a scream. He swung around and saw that the top had been pulled open. Doug's head was poking out and his teeth were bared. The man's hand was bleeding. He lunged at Al with his knife, but Al lifted his sack and the blade slashed it before hitting something hard inside.

'What's this?' one of the actors shouted. 'Intruders? Not in our theatre! Armourer?'

As the word hunters ran, Richard Burbage opened a chest at the side of the stage and started throwing wooden swords to the actors. They pounced and rolled and pulled off one mystifying stage-fighting move after another, fearlessly whacking into the men in grey robes, whose knives were suddenly nowhere near long enough.

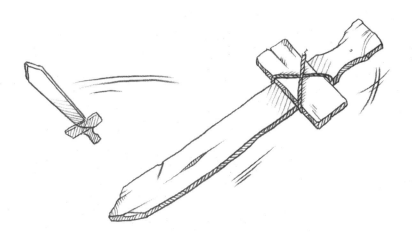

With the attackers taking a pounding and John Johnson having quietly disappeared, the word hunters ran back to the table and the fallen script. The glowing page was face down, but the light came through. Al took the peg from his backpack. There was no time to look for their grandfather here. The men in grey robes had steadied and were taking the fight to the actors.

Lexi opened the portal, Al stuck the peg in, locked it in place and turned the key. A mist rolled across the straw and onto the stage.

In the second that the floor fell away, Al saw them — two men in grey robes diving after him. He kicked. He hit nothing. Then he was falling.

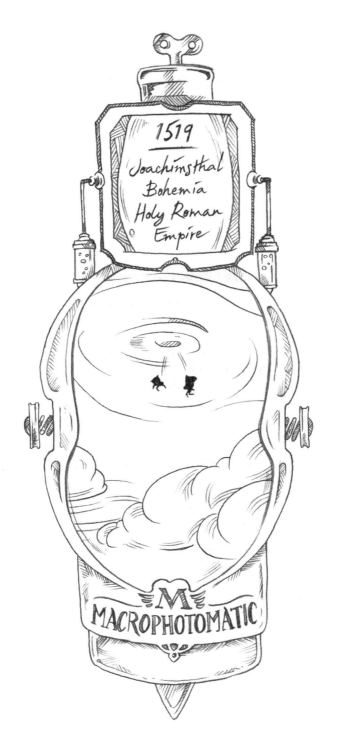

THEY VEERED SIDEWAYS, then struck the turbulence of the Renaissance. Al looked back, but the fog was thick and dark and he couldn't see anything. Then he, Lexi and Will broke free and found themselves in bright daylight. They were falling towards a forest, with a castle on a hill and a town at the foot of it.

'That was them!' Will shouted. 'The men in grey. They know what we're doing. I think they're trying to stop us.'

Al rolled to look back up to the cloud as it started to shrink. Just before it vanished, he noticed two bodies in grey robes drop from it and fall awkwardly.

'Look!' he shouted to the others. 'Fly!'

The word hunters were dropping towards the town, but shaped their arms to swing them away and over the woods, straining to change their course as much as they could. Al glanced behind. The men in grey were tumbling straight down, struggling to work out how to control their fall.

The word hunters crashed through the upper tree branches and dropped to the forest floor. For a moment they said nothing, all three of them turning around and around, checking every tree.

'No one here,' Will said once he was certain of it. 'That's why we need weapons – for dealing with those men most of all.'

'They tried to get into my bag.' Al now had a neatly stitched satchel. They all did. He checked for a slash from the knife, but there wasn't one. Doug was okay, apart from the fresh wee smell.

'They cut mine.' Lexi looked at her satchel. 'It's okay now, but I lost a lot of stuff. My torch broke on the stage and the batteries fell out.'

'They were after the pegs.' Will pointed to Al's satchel. 'This is changing. It's one thing to be on the edge of someone else's battle, but they know exactly who we are and they're coming for us.'

Lexi wanted it not to be true, but the attack seemed planned, as if the men in grey had been waiting for them. 'Well, we know they're here this time. Whatever we're looking for is in the town. We were going to land there. And the town is where they are.'

'Weapons.' Will found a fallen branch and snapped it. 'This is better than nothing until we can find swords or – Where are we? *When* are we?'

They checked the peg.

'Romans?' Lexi took the peg to have a closer look. 'Don't tell me—'

'No.' Al knew what she was thinking. 'It's a thousand years after the Romans. The Holy Roman Empire's a different thing. I know it looks like Teutoburg Forest, but the Romans aren't about to lose three legions here today. We're not here to fight that battle.'

It wasn't just Lexi he wanted to convince. There were

still some nights when he dreamt about that battle and trees
a lot like these. And mud and a man in grey robes on the end
of his borrowed sword.

'We've got money,' Lexi said. Each of them had a cloak
with a hood and an embroidered waistcoat with slashes that
had bright fabric showing through. Their puffy breeches
ended at the knees in yellow leggings. 'And we're not soldiers.
But we all look the same. We look as though we're dressed for
the same thing.'

Never having lived in Bohemia in the early 16th century,
they were not sure what that thing was.

'I hope everyone's dressed like this.' Al looked down at
his legs. 'We'll stand out a bit otherwise. We're in real trouble
if everyone here's in a grey robe.'

They moved off through the trees and stayed well above
the town. The men would be expecting them to go straight
there. The word hunters would find another way in. This was
the last step in 'dollar'. If they could avoid them here, they'd
be home. Lexi still had her picture of Grandad Al in her bag,
though a lot of other things had fallen out. She'd thought
she'd adjusted to being a word hunter. She'd got used to the
job being safer than it first seemed and now it wasn't again.
'Dollar' had been easy and now they were in a forest 500
years from home, with men nearby who seemed to want to
kill them. The stick in her hand wasn't much of an answer
to that.

There were noises ahead – human voices, animals, the
creaking and clanking of wagons on the move. They moved

forward tree by tree, always looking out for the men who had fallen through the portal behind them.

There was a road cut through the forest and they stayed back in the shadows to watch the traffic on it. A heavy wooden cart was being pulled down the mountain by oxen. It had a cover fitted over its heaped cargo and two soldiers on board guarding it. They wore dull steel helmets and olive tunics and had swords on their belts.

'Let's try going away from the town,' Will said. 'Let's see where they're coming from.'

They made their way uphill, keeping to the trees and staying out of sight. They passed two empty carts heading in the same direction. The road ended at a tunnel that had been cut into the hillside, with soldiers surrounding its entrance and checking carts on the way in and out.

As the word hunters watched, a man rode up on a horse.

'He's dressed exactly like us.' Lexi noticed it first. 'That's got to mean something.'

The only difference was the sword they could see beneath his cape.

He spoke to two of the soldiers, dismounted and opened one of the saddlebags on his horse. He took out a piece of parchment with a seal on it and waited while they read it. The soldiers pointed to the mine and back down the road. They were checking something. The man put the document back in his saddlebag. Other guards were called over. They saluted him and escorted him into the tunnel.

One of the two soldiers who had stayed outside led the

man's horse from the entrance and tied its reins to a nearby tree.

'Whatever he was flashing around, it could be good to see it,' Al said. 'Do you think we can get it without them noticing?'

'From above.' Will pointed to a ledge. The hill above the horse was almost a sheer drop. 'We'll use the ropes.'

'And we'll just—' As Lexi started to disagree, she realised she could see some hand or footholds already. There were tree roots, tussocks of grass and places where the rock jutted out. Her father had sent her down tougher slopes when they'd been bushwalking – not that she'd liked it at the time. 'Okay.'

They made their way through the forest and further up the hill before crossing back, until they were directly above the horse. They had a good view of the road and when a cart drew up for inspection, they made their move. They fixed their ropes in place and dropped step-by-step down the slope. Al told himself to treat it like any other steep hillside. Forget the guards, watch his footing, stand out from the rock. And stay quiet.

They made it to the ground safely. Lexi could feel her heart racing. She wondered what she'd say – what Will would say – if a guard stepped out from the tunnel entrance and saw them.

But it didn't happen. No one noticed Will moving to calm the horse or Lexi lifting the document from the saddlebag.

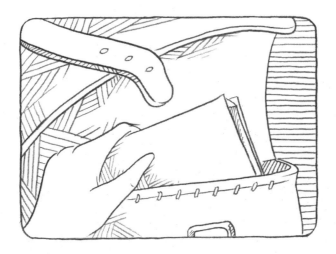

'Take it,' Will whispered. He pointed back up the hill.

Lexi stuck the document in her waistcoat and retraced her footholds, powering back up the slope. She'd always been a good climber – at least as fast as Al – even if climbing was something none of her friends at school rated.

They untied and coiled their ropes and slipped back into the trees.

'I'm impressed,' Will said once they were safe. 'I didn't know you two had been training.'

Lexi felt her cheeks go red as she pulled the document out of her waistcoat. 'Finally I get something out of all those boring trips to national parks with Dad over the years.'

'And there was practically no whingeing this time, which was a nice change.' Al laughed. '"What if my pants get dirty?" "What if I break a nail?" "I don't have a signal."'

'Yeah, well,' she said. 'I wasn't expecting a signal. Just like I wasn't expecting you to beat me to the top. Oh, wait – you didn't.'

The document was a letter signed by a Count Stefan von Schlick appointing Johan Kruger as an inspector of his mines and mint, and requiring all of the count's people to ensure unlimited access.

'So that's the mine,' Al said. 'And it's mining whatever metal they're using to make the coins in the mint. The mint has to be the place and it's got to be in the town. Someone's got to say something about dollars there.'

He looked for the town through the trees, but couldn't see it. He could make out the next ridge line, which was also covered in forest. He had one peg left, so 'dollar' had to begin here, in this valley, at this time.

'So,' Lexi said to Will, 'how do you feel about being Johan Kruger and getting us into the mint?'

'What if he's already been there?' Al took a closer look at the letter. 'They might even know him.'

Will thought about it. 'Lexi's right. I think *you're* right to say the mint's going to be it, but they don't make mints easy to get into. If we're lucky this gets us in the front door. The seal should get us through. We look like the real deal and a lot of these people can't read.'

Al didn't want to think about what would happen if they could read and if they'd known Johan Kruger for years. He had no better plan. And he figured he'd lose a vote if the three of them were a democracy. Which he wasn't at all sure they were. There hadn't been a boss before Will came along. Before *they* saved *him* in 1839. They'd saved him at the Globe, too. Much as Al told himself there was no point in keeping that kind of tally, he seemed to be keeping one anyway. But Will would be good to have around in any fight that came up, and without him the attack at the Globe might have ended very differently.

The town was even smaller than they had first thought. As they left the trees, they watched for the men in grey robes. It might be easy to lose them in a city, but not here. They dropped the sticks at the edge of the forest, since Johan Kruger and his clerks wouldn't carry them.

'We've got nothing,' Lexi said. 'Just bare hands to take on those guys. And Johan Kruger's going to come out of that mine sometime and he'll probably have to show his letter to someone.'

'So we move fast.' Will was already leading the way between two houses. 'That's all we can do.'

From the street the layout of the town was clearer. At its centre it had a church, a timber yard and a large building next to it that was heavily guarded and had to be the mint. It had a solid wooden door with metal bands across it and, along one side, an equally solid gate. There were only a few small windows and they were far above street level. Further back there were chimneys, putting out white smoke.

A cart arrived. Its covers were lifted, its load inspected and the gate was opened for it to go in. But the only way for Johan Kruger was through the front door.

They checked the doorways and shutters of the houses as they passed, always ready for the men in grey robes. They watched the forest's edge, but it was too easy to believe there might be anything in there, hidden in the dark and moving with them.

When they came to the small town square, they crossed it the way the count's men would – confidently, as if they were one step removed from the guy who owned the place. The soldiers at the door held poles in their hands that ended in broad silver blades and each of them wore a sword.

As they looked at the letter, something made Lexi turn around. Across the square, between two houses, she saw the grey-robed men ducking back into the shadows.

'They're here,' she said quietly to Al. 'Don't look.'

There was no safer place for the word hunters to be than surrounded by soldiers, but they had been seen. The men knew where they were.

Al stared straight ahead, knowing that there were people nearby who wanted to attack him and who were watching him, and all he could do was wait for Will to persuade the guards that three inspectors with one letter was not so unusual.

The door was opened for them to go in and then bolted behind them by one of two more guards who were in the first room. A clerk checked the letter and recorded their arrival in a book.

'It's good to meet you, Mr Kruger,' he said. 'I'd heard the count had a new inspector. I'm glad to see you're escorted. As our reputation grows, the forest roads are becoming less safe. Please—' He indicated the doorway behind him, which led further into the building. 'I'll leave you to your business.'

Beyond it was a corridor and this time there were no guards.

'We got lucky,' Will said before the others could speak. 'Looks like they've got quite a system. Let's move before the real Johan gets here. It's good he's not on your mum and dad's fleet plan. He'd be on the phone already.'

'What are we looking for?' Al wanted to focus on 'dollar' and then a way out. 'I don't think this is one where we can look for Grandad.'

Lexi wanted him to be wrong, but the risks were too great.

'We inspect things,' Will said. 'We make our way around the building. We go anywhere anyone might say whatever we need to hear and we get them to say it as soon as possible. Then we go.'

On the ground floor, the cart that had arrived was being emptied of its load. A sack of rubble was opened for them to check. A rock was taken out and held up to the light of a candle so that they could see a seam of silver gleaming in it.

The room was hot and the horses edgy at being kept in there. It backed onto a stone wall around furnaces, where timber fires burnt to melt the silver from the crushed rock.

They climbed a flight of stairs and looked down on the furnaces as molten silver ran along a channel and into a stone basin the size of a bath, where impurities were skimmed from the surface.

'Hey, that's like Caractacus,' Will said, 'though way bigger, obviously.'

'Inspectors,' a voice said from a level above. They were immediately on their guard. 'I'd heard you were in the building.' They looked up and saw a small man with dark hair looking down at them. 'I'm Karl Sachs. I'm the one you're looking for.'

'Excellent.' Will moved towards the stairs. Karl Sachs had something for them to inspect, whatever it was.

Al and Lexi followed and Karl Sachs met them at the top.

'Let me take you somewhere a little cooler.' He indicated the door he'd come out of. 'Some of our best work is done in there.'

He led them into an open workshop area. At one bench, blank coins were being tipped from moulds and checked for weight. One of the men there took a blank, cut it in two and started to re-melt it in a small cup.

'The blank coins need to be the exact weight and size,' Karl Sachs explained. 'They also need to be nine-tenths silver and we melt one down every so often to check its composition. It's these standards that have people talking about our work here.' He was clearly proud of it and glad to be giving new inspectors the tour.

Next he took them to two men who were working on thick discs of metal. One was cutting down into his with fine tools, stopping after every movement to check his work. The other had a hammer and a small steel rod, which he was striking against the design he was working on. The discs were the dies that would be used to punch the coins and, even though they were made of steel, each one lost the sharpness of its image within a few days and had to be replaced.

There were large pictures of both sides of the coin on the wall behind their work bench. One was of a bearded man with a robe and a halo and the other was of a lion, taken, Karl Sachs said, from the count's crest.

On the other side of the workshop, a row of men made coins. Each blank was fitted between a pair of dies and the dies struck exactly hard enough with a hammer so that the blank became a perfectly marked coin. A supervisor walked up and down the far side of the bench picking up coins at random, taking them to a small window and checking each side closely with a magnifying glass before placing the coin back on the table. A younger man scooped finished coins into a wooden box.

'The minters are good,' Karl Sachs said. 'There's an art to it. But however good they are, some coins are not quite what they should be. So they need to be checked.'

'One hundred.' The man with the coin box stood up straight and stepped away from the bench.

Karl Sachs waved him over, reached into the box and lifted out a bright new coin.

'The lion must be just right.' He studied one side closely before turning it over. 'Saint Joachim must be just right or the coin is melted down again. Look at it. It's beautiful.' He held the coin out so that they could see the detail. 'And to think that to some people it's just money. Do you know what they're starting to call them?' He set the coin back down in

the box as if it needed careful handling. 'They might all be great guilders, but ours stand out. People are giving them their own name now. Joachimsthal – the valley of Saint Joachim – is the home of the Joachimsthaler.'

Al wanted to tell him that there was more to come. His coins would change the languages of Europe. The 'thaler' from 'Joachimsthaler' would become 'daalder' and 'dollar', and hundreds of years later the dollar would be one of the most common currencies in the world.

As the man with the coin box fitted the lid into place, gold light pulsed from the Joachimsthaler Karl Sachs had shown them.

Lexi stepped forward. 'Could we take a close look at that?'

'You can look at anything,' Karl Sachs said. 'You're the inspectors.' There was a clicking sound as the lid of the box closed and the pins of a lock moved into place. The glow of the portal was gone. 'All the coins are alike, though. They have to be. Any one's as good as another.'

He picked up a coin from the table, gave it to Lexi and signalled for the man with the box to keep moving.

'Thank you.' Lexi made it look as though she was studying the coin closely. 'It's a very fine piece of work.' She pointed to the box. 'Where does that go next?'

It was being weighed on a set of scales, checked to see that it was exactly the same weight as a box of blank coins.

'To the floor below.' Karl Sachs watched as the box was lifted from the scales and carried away. 'That's the last we'll see of them. There's a treasury room there. They're taken out in those boxes.'

'That's where we're to go next.' Will reached out to shake Karl Sachs's hand. 'You do excellent work here. No wonder the count's so pleased. I'm sorry our visit has to be so brief. We have to leave with enough daylight—'

'Ah, the road through the forest, yes.' Karl Sachs nodded. 'Make sure you're out the other side of it before the sun sets.'

The man carrying the box was moving quickly. He was already on the stairs. The word hunters went after him, wanting to run, but knowing they couldn't.

They took the steps two at a time. Will was at the front and so focused on moving quickly that he didn't see the spade swing at him as he reached the bottom, or the man in grey who stepped from the shadows. The spade struck his shoulder and he fell to the floor.

Al jumped the railing onto the head of Will's attacker. He gouged his eyes, and the man screamed. Al choked him and the man grabbed at his hands. Lexi caught the spade as he dropped it and swung it up just as the second man in grey brought his spade down like an axe towards Will's head. His spade struck hers with a clang and deflected away, hitting the wooden floor and getting stuck between two planks. The man charged at Lexi before she could lift her spade again, but Will stood, got his good shoulder under him and flipped the man over the railing.

One ankle caught on a post and he scrambled to grab something – anything – as he fell backwards. His arms flailed and he plummeted into the bath of molten silver. There was a terrible scream and then he was silent.

Will took the spade from Lexi and smashed it into the knee of the man in grey who was battling with Al. The man fell, grabbed his leg and writhed around on the floor. Al stepped away from him.

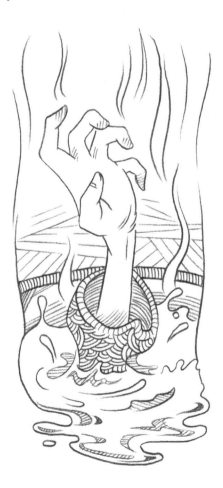

'Let's go,' Will said. 'He's not coming after us.' There was a corridor ahead. It was the only way the man with the box could have gone. 'We're all right. We've got the letter from the count. As far as the guards know, those men broke in.'

They could hear guards running below them, drawn to the noise.

There was an open door further along the corridor with a soldier on it. He had his sword in his hand and was looking their way. Will ran towards him, holding the letter out.

'Count's inspectors,' he shouted. 'We've been attacked. There are intruders in the building.' He pointed back down the corridor. 'That way! That way!'

The guard took a step and then stopped. 'But this is my post.'

'Go!' Will held the letter closer to his face. 'That's an order on the count's authority.'

There was more noise downstairs as the guard hurried along the corridor. Someone shouted at the entrance to the building. A bell rang. Around the building, more bells joined in.

'Intruders!' someone outside shouted. 'They're dressed as inspectors and have the count's letter.'

Johan Kruger had arrived.

The word hunters ran through the treasury doorway. The man who had brought the box was setting it on a shelf with dozens of others. Will shouted to him to step away.

He lifted his hands and took a pace back. He bumped into a table and reached down to balance himself.

Will took the box and smashed it onto the floor. The lid split and coins spilt out – 99 regular Joachimsthalers and one with a glowing gold 'home' portal.

Lexi saw it and jumped on it. Al was already finding the peg. There were guards in the corridor, running towards them.

Lexi opened the portal and the three of them moved to the far corner of the room. Al drove the peg in. As he locked it in place, guards appeared in the doorway with swords in their hands.

Al turned the key. Mist rose up through the floor and poured in through the doorway. The floorboards shuddered, the walls shook and the word hunters lifted away. They saw soldiers in the square and then the town grew small – a pale gap in the dark forest and then a speck.

Centuries of light and dark passed as the earth spun below. They hadn't found their grandfather. But they were alive.

The spinning slowed and the fall to earth began. Below them the land met an ocean, a river wound its way through a city, a creek passed through a leafy suburb, traffic moved on the streets at exactly its usual speed and the word hunters landed in the park next to Mursili and the dictionary.

'You've got to watch those branches,' Mursili said to Al. 'You nearly collected one on the way past.'

Al looked down, to make sure that he was back in his own clothes. 'That's the least of our worries.'

Will winced as he pulled up the sleeve of his T-shirt. The welt from the spade had a clear edge to it where it reached his arm, and it extended under his shirt and across his back. The tip of his shoulder felt tender where the bone had been struck.

'We have enemies,' he said to Mursili. They had dropped their guard at the mint. They had assumed they were past the men in grey and their minds had been only on the portal. 'It's my own fault. I should have been looking. Al and Lexi stopped them from killing me.'

'Who are they, though?' Lexi couldn't help looking around, scanning the park. Dogs were being walked. There were kids in the playground. She wanted a weapon. As the breeze blew through the trees, the shadows moved.

'I don't know.' Will wished he had a better answer. 'All I know is they're out there. And it's good that there are three of us.'

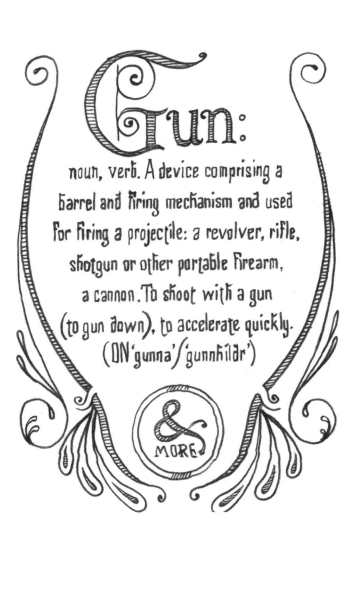

# Gun:

noun, verb. A device comprising a barrel and firing mechanism and used for firing a projectile: a revolver, rifle, shotgun or other portable firearm, a cannon. To shoot with a gun (to gun down), to accelerate quickly. (ON 'gunna' / 'gunnhildr')

& MORE

IT CERTAINLY WASN'T the word Lexi wanted to see. Al came to her door the following Sunday afternoon, while she was downloading some new music. She knew from the look on his face that the time had come again.

'What is it?' She was putting a new playlist together, but she dropped the song. 'What's the word?'

'It's "gun".' He held his hand up. 'Don't go assuming anything. It might be okay. "Water" was a nightmare, remember, so you can never tell.'

They sent a text to Will and Mursili.

Will's reply came through within a minute. 'Good one. Done it before. Not as bad as some. Don't be alarmed by it being "gun".'

As she waited with Al in the park, Lexi could instantly come up with 50 ways it could become a disaster.

'"Not as bad as some"?' She scrolled through Will's text message, for at least the tenth time. 'How bad is that? He once fought a million Aztecs while he had gastro and they wanted to sacrifice him alive. It's *gun*. It's not a word that got invented at a flower show.'

'Yeah. Just so you know, I didn't pick it.' In his own head, Al was workshopping at least another 50 ways it could turn ugly. 'It's the history of the word, not the weapon, so—'

'Yeah, and one time, long ago and far away from any wars, this peaceful shepherd was in a meadow, putting together his entry for the competition to name a brand new weapon that goes bang and shoots people. So we turn up, pat a few sheep, watch him write "G-U-N" on the entry form, poke in the peg and come home.' She glared in the direction of the bus stop. 'Does that sound likely?'

'Well, soon we'll know. Will can actually tell us with this one. That's got to be good. He'll know what the risks are. And where we have to be and when.' It made sense when he said it, even if he didn't feel it. 'He got through it last time without knowing all that.'

'And that means it's okay he's the boss, right? I know you know history, but he's, like, practically 20 and smart and he's done at least 50 words, including this one. So we have to—'

'It's probably hard to think straight when you've got such a massive crush on him.' Al was already irritated that Will kept behaving like he was the boss. He didn't need Lexi making it official.

'I don't have a—' She put her hands up to cover her face. She could feel it burning. 'Just supposing I did, which I don't, do you think he'd know?'

'I think his mind's on the job. And I don't think there's a boss, but it would be smart for us to take his lead on this one, because he's done it before.'

A bus turned the corner and pulled up. Mursili was the second person off. He could see them waiting under the trees and headed in their direction.

'So, interesting one,' he said when he got closer. He sounded enthusiastic about it. Which was easy, since he wasn't going. 'If only we'd had a few guns when the Kaskians attacked Hattusa. We would have handed them back their bottoms in large ceramic vessels for the storage of beverages.' He stopped and sighed. 'That is so disappointing in translation. Much punchier in Hittite. It's a famous phrase of ours when you want to be a little bold about your intended treatment of an adversary. The vessel is "palhi" and don't even ask how I would've translated "arraz".' Lexi and Al didn't seem as interested as he'd hoped. 'But now's not the time for a lesson in Hittite. "Gun." I've looked it up.' He scrolled through notes on his phone. 'It's an odd one. Old Norse, so, Vikings. I can't see any sign of steps to get there and if Vikings had guns Wikipedia's got a lot of rewriting to do. And they're not alone.'

Al showed him the page in the dictionary. The wording fitted with what Mursili had said, but it told them nothing more.

'"Gunna", "Gunnhildr". I'll be interested to hear how it started with them.' Mursili almost put his finger on the portal before Al pulled the book back. 'Sorry. I – It'd be awful to send you there without Will. Though my archery skills might be handy.'

'Do you want to—'

'Oh, no, I don't think so. You need someone, um – I'm the guy in the control room with the screens, remember? I'm all about the information. I'm a googler, not a fighter.' He looked uncomfortable. 'But I'm tempted, of course.'

Behind Mursili, Lexi could see another bus pulling up. Will waved as he stepped off with his backpack over one shoulder.

'I have good news and bad news,' he said as he stopped next to Mursili to hook his other arm into his backpack. It sounded as if he was telling an old joke. 'The good news is there's only three steps to go through. The bad news is I'm pretty sure we'll meet our friends in grey at the first one. But I got past them last time and I can do it again. And this time we've got the three of us and—' He stopped there. 'One of the stages is a party. A celebration. A couple are a bit rough, but let's just go. I'll brief you when we get to each one.'

He gave his injured shoulder a stretch. It was feeling much better. The bruising had tracked down to his elbow, but it was starting to fade.

Mursili stepped back from the dictionary.

'What are you not telling us?' Lexi said to Will.

But Al had touched the button and a bank of mist was already rolling up from the creek.

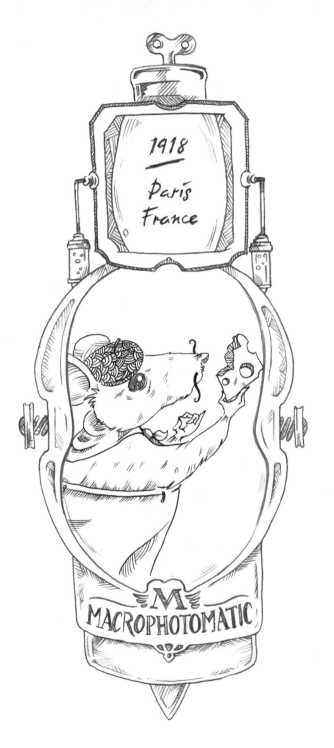

**W**ILL'S GOOD NEWS was wrong.

He braced himself for a drop of centuries, but they burst into daylight much earlier, after a few small bumps.

Below them lay a city with a river passing through it and public gardens with paths meeting at circular beds. There were square palaces with central courtyards and two islands crossed by streets that continued on either bank into the distance, into the suburbs.

The word hunters landed on the riverbank, on a quay opposite stone buildings with blue-black roofs.

'This is Paris,' Will said as he took it all in. 'I've seen pictures. What year is it? You've got to tell me.'

As Al reached for the peg, Lexi checked what she was wearing.

'Yay!' She twirled to show off her dress. 'It's "gun" and I'm dressed like a girl, not like a soldier.' She even had a parasol. They were all civilians. 'I wish I'd got the backpack, though. These picnic baskets are cute, but—'

'I knew it.' Will took the peg from Al and showed her the year. 'It's my time. This is Paris in my time. London's just—' He turned and made a guess, pointing roughly downstream – 'over there.'

As Lexi watched Will looking around at Paris, at an era that he understood and a place not far from his home, she felt sick. She wondered how soon he would leave them. They had landed late in the greatest war in history, they had barely started on the mission and the word was 'gun'. She couldn't bear the thought of him going now, but this was what they'd promised him. Caractacus or 1918.

Will took off his hat and read the label inside. 'The hats are Homburgs,' he said, mainly to Al, who was wearing one too. 'And what we're wearing on our legs are spats. I know this stuff. I don't usually get to – We're pretty stylish, you and me. This isn't what I wear at home.' He put the hat back on his head and smiled. 'Paris. In 1918. I always wanted to come to Paris.'

But something was going on that didn't fit with the Paris he'd imagined. Near them on the quay, men and women were gathering around a hole. Something had blasted it a metre deep into the stone, and rubble and other debris were scattered across the cobbles. A few of the people were looking up at the sky, which was clear and blue.

'There was no plane,' a man was saying, as if his word was being questioned. 'There was nothing.'

'Do they already have guns in Paris?' another voice said. 'Or something that can fly so high we can't see it?'

There was a crash and a boom somewhere nearby, behind the riverfront buildings. On the quay, people screamed and ran, though they had no idea where to go. Some held their hands over their heads. One woman lost her hat and it rolled like a wheel before tipping over.

'I've got it,' Will said. 'I didn't do this one when I did "gun". I read about it in the papers. I'd already done "gun" by then. It's March 1918, the Germans are beginning their spring offensive and the biggest gun the world has ever seen, the Kaiser Wilhelm, is parked in a forest a long way north of here. This is the morning it's started shelling Paris.' They could see smoke above the quayside buildings and hear the bells of fire engines. 'You realise that's where we've got to go? To the gun. That's how this one works. It's a bunch of famous guns with names. I just didn't know Kaiser Bill would be on the list. I know how to do the rest of them.'

'But you—' Lexi stopped herself. It sounded like Will was coming with them, at least for now. She'd expected him to leave – to tell them what they needed to know about the stages ahead and set off for London.

'I'm the best guide you'll get to 1918.' He knew what she was thinking. 'And to this gun. Even if I've never seen it before.'

He watched a boat drifting down the river, a man selling magazines. He had always wanted to come to Paris, but not like this. In the 21st century he had googled it and worked out exactly which cabarets he would see after the war. He would come in 1921, when they rebuilt the Moulin Rouge.

He had googled the war, too, and knew it would be over in November. But today there would be panic on the streets of Paris. Panic was exactly what the Kaiser Wilhelm was for. It was a huge gun, but not much of a weapon in terms of the damage it could do. All it had going for it was distance and secrecy. It could send small shells a long way without much accuracy, but as long as they kept landing in the middle of Paris the fear in the city would build.

'We need a pilot,' he told the others. 'It's spotted by a pilot.'

'And what do we do with him when we get him?' Al couldn't see what good a pilot would do them. 'Tell him where it is and then what?'

'We get him to take us to the gun.' Will tried to make it sound as though it wasn't a big deal. There were two armies and a war between them and the Kaiser Wilhelm. 'It's a lot smarter than going through the battlefront.'

Al knew he was right about avoiding the battlefront. At school he'd seen film from the time and there had been movies about it on TV, with endless mud and rubble and smashed trees. Barbed wire, explosions, gas. No one had planned for how bad it would be.

'So how do we get the pilot to take us?' It didn't seem as straightforward to Al as Will had put it. 'I'm guessing it's not a thing they do regularly – take civilians up in the air and drop them behind enemy lines.'

'The pilot who finds the gun will be a hero,' Lexi said. 'That's what we've got to bargain with. If Will knows where the gun is.'

'But what do we do when we get there?'

'We can't solve everything now.' Will could picture the gun on rail tracks, but that was all. He thought it was based in a tunnel. 'It'll be the portal. And the Germans will hear us in fluent German. We need to get close and then find a way in. And we need to get moving now. There'll be another shell in a few minutes.'

Will turned towards the steps that led up to the street. Al wanted more answers, a more detailed plan. They were about to fly into a war and then work out what to do next. He wanted to be home. He wanted a different word. He'd read too many of the last letters that soldiers had sent back from this war. Every country town in Australia had its war memorial to its World War I dead.

His shoe caught in his spats and he stumbled on the steps. And noticed the initials written on the stone in blue ballpoint pen. 'AH'.

He grabbed Lexi's arm. 'Look!'

She read the letters. 'Hey, one of the – It's 1918, so it's a word hunter from *after* 1918. It's—'

'From the 1940s or later. First commercial ballpoint pen – Argentina, 1943, Laszlo Biro. I looked it up. And next to the initials – that wiggly line and the thing beside it. If you're from 1918 it's nothing, but if you're from after 1970—'

'It's the Sydney Opera House and the Harbour Bridge. It's Grandad Al. He's been here.' Lexi set her basket on a step and looked down at the people on the quay. 'He might still be here.'

Paris was a big city. She didn't know where to start with their photos. But they had a trace of him. And if he was here he would be in a Homburg hat and spats, a civilian.

There were soldiers on the street when they reached the top of the steps from the quay. Despite the two explosions, they were smoking and laughing together. They were on leave, most of them, taking their turn away from the front.

There were American and British soldiers as well as French. There were probably Australians, too. They were writing postcards on the quay and drinking coffee in cafes. One of them was playing a trumpet. The word hunters showed their photo around, but no one recognised Grandad Al. Somewhere in the distance another shell landed.

Will found a group of French pilots sitting outside a cafe. He knew what to look for. The war had been going since he was 11, and he'd memorised all the uniforms, medals and weapons of the allied armies. The French pilots' uniform was so dark it was almost black. It had a golden wing sewn at each end of the collar opening back from a star, and a pair of wings crossed by a propeller on each sleeve. The pants were baggy at the top and tucked into boots that came to just below the knees.

One of the pilots was showing with his hands the angle he had used to attack a German plane and bring it down. He was talking as if he was the expert, but the others kept interrupting and telling him what he should have done. They were all telling bigger and better stories about what heroes they were. At the edge of the group one pilot sat looking far less interested than the rest.

The man next to him nudged him and said, 'Don't worry, Didier. One day they'll give you a gun.'

'I have a gun.' He sounded irritated. 'I have three guns. I'm in a Salmson 2.'

'I'm sure it's still important work,' the other man said, smirking. 'Even if you never get to fire them. We need people who can – what is it you do? Fly over things and look at them?'

The others laughed.

'We have a huge army that would hardly know what to shoot at if I didn't tell them.' Didier thumped the arm of his chair. 'It *is* important work.' That only brought more laughter. 'I'm going to get more coffee.'

He pushed his chair back, stood up and walked inside. The word hunters followed.

Lexi took the photo of Grandad Al from her basket. 'Have you seen this man?'

Didier glanced at the photo. 'With that foolish hat? In Paris? I don't think so.' He tried to attract the attention of the staff, but they were looking the other way. He tapped a coin on the counter.

Al felt scuffling in his backpack as Doug clambered to the top, smelling buttery pastry, dark chocolate, almonds, sugar. He stepped back and swung his pack down, holding the flap shut. He found a broken corner of croissant on the floor and posted it under the flap.

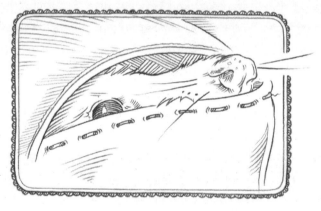

'That's it,' he whispered. 'That's all they've got here. People have eaten the rest.'

Will stepped up to the counter next to Didier. 'I agree it's important work, finding the targets. The most important.'

Didier looked him up and down. What he saw was a man who could fight, but who wasn't in uniform. 'And why should I care about what you think?'

'Only one reason,' Will said. 'The shells landing on Paris today are coming from a gun a long way north of the city. Someone will be a hero for locating it exactly. We can take you to it. You can be the one who finds it.'

Didier looked doubtful. 'We? I take three people up in my Salmson for a tour of the front because you tell me – when no one else in Paris has any idea – that you know exactly what's going on out there? Why should I—'

'Because we've come through the lines near Soissons this morning. We know where the gun is. We were bringing the news to General Petain, but the Germans launched a new offensive at dawn and he's left the city.' Will could remember it well. It was 21 March and Jack Campbell from three doors down his street was last seen that morning, at the start of the biggest bombardment of the war. 'I can either give this information to a colonel, who will give it to someone else, who will—' He shrugged. 'Or I can find someone who can act on it now.'

Didier nodded. 'Some of those colonels do a lot of talking.'

At that moment another shell landed just down the street. The glass in the cafe windows shook. Debris blew past outside. Women screamed and the pilots at the tables ducked.

'Let the colonels talk,' Lexi said. 'Someone has to do something. Before too many people are hurt, before there's too much panic. Paris will celebrate the pilot who stops it.'

Didier thought about it for a second. 'I'll do it for Paris, not for any celebration.' He put his coin back in his pocket. 'Do you know how easy it is to get a medal for shooting down planes and how hard it is to get one for spotting targets? Don't people know that the bullets the Germans shoot at you are just the same?'

Didier was their man.

He didn't even talk to the other pilots on his way out. The word hunters followed him to the street, where he stepped in front of the traffic and held up a hand.

'I am commandeering this truck for the war effort,' he said to the driver who had stopped a few centimetres in front of him.

They had an argument about the importance of the truck driver's potatoes to the war effort, but Didier waved the word hunters on board even as the driver was speaking. They climbed up and crouched among the potato sacks, while Didier sat in front and gave the driver far more directions than he needed.

They passed through the suburbs of Paris, through markets and streets crowded with houses and then past gardens and farms and patches of forest. As they came to a high wire fence a plane flew overhead, just above the treetops. It looked no sturdier than a box kite and sounded like a lawn mower.

For Al it was like coming face to face with World War I for the first time. Paris had been Paris, despite the soldiers and the shelling, but there in the sky was a man off to war this minute, peering through his goggles and past his machine gun. Soon the word hunters would be up there, too, and maybe on their way to Grandad Al. He'd heard of the long-range German guns, but couldn't recall seeing a picture, in books or online or among Grandad Al's sketches.

'Hey!' He bumped Lexi's knee. 'Grandad Al never drew this.' There were plenty of drawings they'd found that Al still couldn't place – bearded kings, ships with two rows of oars, crumbling chapels, odd devices – but none of artillery pieces. 'There's no picture at home of the Kaiser Wilhelm or any other big gun. But we know he came here.'

'He didn't draw everything.' Lexi thought about it. 'Maybe he didn't get home from this one. Maybe this is it.' For a second, the idea of finding Grandad Al had never seemed more real. Then she saw another plane through the fence, bumping along the ground, taxiing on its way to take off. On its way to the war. 'I hope he's okay.'

She imagined him shot down on his flight to the gun, or lost in the trenches, or captured by the Germans. She tried to force those thoughts from her head. There was no limit to the bad things that might have happened, but they needed to hope they hadn't. They were going to a war again and they needed to get that right to have any chance of finding Grandad Al.

The guards at the gate saluted Didier, when they saw him in the cab of the truck. The driver hardly slowed down. Didier made him take them all the way to his plane, before letting him get back to delivering his potatoes.

The ease of it made no sense to Lexi and Al. There was a war close by, but there were far fewer security checks than they would have to go through just to get to Sydney in the 21st century. The guards knew Didier, though, and he was an officer and that seemed to be enough.

Didier's plane looked to Al like a classic World War I biplane. Its wings were joined by struts and wires, its wheels looked like they had come from a wheelbarrow and the shape of the bones of its wooden frame could be seen through the canvas that had been stretched over it. It hardly looked safe to fly at all. It looked like a mad inventor had built it out of verandah railings, a Hills hoist and a shopping trolley.

Lexi stopped and stared at it. 'Seriously?'

Will had already walked over to it. 'It's a fine-looking machine.' He put his hand up to the canvas. 'These are new, aren't they?'

'Late last year.' Didier stroked the wooden propeller with his gloved hand. 'This one's three weeks old. They replaced the Dorand. We sold those to the Americans.' He laughed. 'These are 40 kilometres an hour faster. You can almost see that just to look at it. Good with a load as well.'

He turned around to size up Lexi and Al. He looked like he was calculating something. 'We'll have you two instead of bombs. It'll work. Fuel, ammunition, the four of us, yes. All under 500 kilos. The tall one gets the gunner's seat. And navigates. You'd better be serious about knowing where this thing is.'

'Don't worry, I know.' Will was looking up at the cockpit. 'Are those Lewis guns with the cooling shroud taken off? Am I going to get to use them?'

'Maybe. Maybe not.' Didier treated it as if it was no big deal. 'You'll need to watch for fighters. See? This job takes courage after all.'

'So we're—' Al wasn't looking forward to being boxed up inside.

'Inside, yes.' Didier indicated the lower part of the fuselage.

'I'm really better if I see the horizon.'

'He's no good either way,' Lexi said. 'And Will knows where we're going.'

Didier held out his hand for her so that she could climb onto the wing and into the rear cockpit. She ducked down and moved forward, as he told her to, and wedged herself and her basket between the two seats. Al climbed in next and lowered himself feet first into the fuselage behind the gunner's seat. The plane narrowed the further back he went and he knew he'd never get comfortable on the timber and nuts and bolts. Then Will's feet came in and went either side of his head.

'Loving the plan so far,' Al said to Will's right foot, moving his arm just enough to give a thumbs-up.

Didier called a mechanic over and even inside the body of the plane they could feel him swinging the propeller to get it started. On the fourth try the engine coughed into life and the entire plane started to vibrate. Al felt every bump as Didier opened up the engine and the plane stumbled and then rushed across the ground. Their heads rang with the noise of the engine and the air smelt of burnt fuel.

There was a lurch and they were up.

Lexi and Al could just make out Will shouting at Didier and telling him to go north. They knew they were over allied territory at first, but there was no way to know when that had changed. Didier had given Will a map and from time to time Will shouted directions about following a train line or a road, or looking out for a particular town.

Will kept twisting in his seat to look at the ground ahead so that he could make sense of where they were. Every time he did it he was conscious that he wasn't looking out behind them for enemy fighters. He tried to remember precisely what they looked like from front on and how to tell them from British, French or American planes. He swung his machine guns around lining clouds up in the sights.

In the fuselage Al's face started to feel numb in the cold air and the plane's vibrations hummed right through him. The plane tilted and swayed. Al's stomach lurched. He focused on his breathing, imagined a horizon and tried not to think about vomiting.

About half an hour had passed when Will looked down between his feet and shouted, 'Nearly there!' He turned around and called something out to Didier.

Al and Lexi couldn't hear it properly, but they could make out enough to know it was the next part of the plan. He wanted Didier to land when they were near the gun. He would only tell him where it was if Didier would land nearby and let them out.

'It's madness!' Didier shouted over his shoulder.

Will half-turned to the front. 'Do you mean you can't do it?'

'Of course I can do it. I could do it in my sleep. The madness is being dropped behind enemy lines for no good reason.' There was a pause as he checked the sky ahead. 'But it's your madness, and if you want to be so mad—' He shrugged. 'I just want to find the gun. For Paris.'

'Try 30 degrees to the right.' The edges of the map flapped as Will held a protractor up to it. 'Look for a forested hill with a chateau just beyond it.'

Suddenly there was a crash in the air near them, then another. Smoke blew by. It was anti-aircraft fire coming from the ground.

'I see it,' Didier shouted. 'The hill's just ahead. Three hundred metres. The gun's firing over it. Mark it.'

Will put a cross on the map. Didier dipped the plane to get out of the line of fire. There was another crash, much closer, and something punched through the canvas in front of Al's face and passed straight through the other side of the plane. Sunlight and air rushed through the two holes, neither of them bigger than his thumb.

Will stuck his head down into the fuselage. 'Landing!'

Lexi and Al braced themselves. The plane hit the road and bounced, then bounced again and rolled to a stop. Al's stomach heaved around and he put one hand over his mouth.

'Quickly!' Didier shouted. He kept the engine running. The plane was straining to pull forward.

Will jumped out and Al followed.

As Lexi handed him her basket, he said, 'See, I didn't even—' and vomited on the side of the plane.

Inside his bag Doug vomited, too.

Lexi clambered down past them with her skirts hitched up to her knees. Her hat was back in the plane.

There was a field on one side of the road and a forest on the other. They ran for the trees. Didier revved the engine and the plane shot off down the road and up into the sky.

From the forest the word hunters could hear more explosions, but they could hear the plane's engine, too. It didn't miss a beat. The explosions stopped. The noise of the engine grew fainter and fainter as Didier headed south. Al crouched down and took a few deep breaths of the fresh forest air.

'Nice one.' Lexi patted him on the shoulder. 'I think Didier can charge you a 60-dollar cleaning fee for that.'

They moved further into the forest and up a low hill. The trees thinned out near the top, enough to give them a clear view of the road they had landed on. It was empty.

Al took a step to the right so that he could see further. 'I thought they might be searching for us.'

'Yeah.' Will was listening for trucks, but he couldn't hear any. 'I don't know if they realise we landed. They might think Didier ducked behind the hill to avoid the firing.'

A loud boom rang out and the ground shook. The noise seemed to echo, or there were smaller versions of it almost immediately from other parts of the forest. The word hunters dropped to their knees.

'That'll be it,' Will said. 'That's Kaiser Bill.'

They stood up and moved forward. From the top of the hill they could see the barrel of a gun rising like the mast of a ship over the next hill and above the trees. It was thinner than Al had expected. It didn't look like something that would terrorise a city.

'So, how do we get there?' He looked for soldiers, but didn't see any. 'I'm guessing they won't make this next bit easy for us.'

'Or maybe they will.' Lexi had seen something. She pointed through the trees. There was a door set into the hillside and it looked new.

It opened as they watched and two German sailors came out. One of them was putting on a coat.

'It's been developed from a naval gun,' Will said. 'Those sailors have got to be something to do with it. There's no other reason for German sailors to come out of that door. It'll be their barracks. They've dug it into the hillside so they can't be seen from the air.'

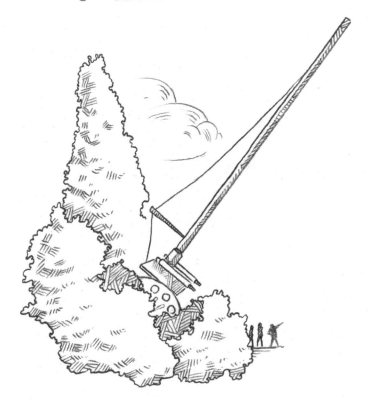

'Oh, I thought it might be a smart way to the gun.' Just as that idea went nowhere, Lexi had another. 'They'll have uniforms in there. We can be German sailors.'

'Great,' Will said. 'Great idea. Though maybe you should try to keep the talking to a minimum, since you'll probably sound like a German girl rather than a German sailor.'

'Don't they have—' She stopped herself. 'No, I guess they don't. In the future they have women in the navy, just so you know. But I'll keep quiet.'

'You're also 12. I don't want to make a big deal of that but – Yeah, don't talk. And try to look like a teenager. You need to look like a 15-year-old guy at least.' With Lexi dressed like a French girl, it wasn't easy for Will to picture. 'It's lucky you're tall. Try to look big. And make sure you're at the back.'

They made their way through the trees towards the door, ready to duck down into the bushes if it opened again. It didn't. Al wanted a better plan, a less risky way to the gun. He knew how both sides treated spies in World War I and it wasn't good.

Al stopped Will as he was about to move to the door. 'If there's anyone there, tell them you've just been transferred here. You got the call when you were on leave and your kit's coming from Kiel. You need to borrow someone's to go on duty today.'

'Good.' Will nodded. 'Nice detail.'

'And keep it simple. You're just a seaman. One of the crew. No special skills.'

'I could—' Will stopped himself. 'Yeah. And no war stories either. I was going to say I fought at the Battle of Jutland, but – No, simple's the way to go.'

He stood up, straightened his coat, walked confidently to the door and pushed it open. Behind it was a long room with bare rock walls and bunk beds. Each one had a trunk at the end of it and several of the sailors' black jackets were hanging on a rope that someone had tied between two of the beds.

He waved to Lexi and Al.

'Uniforms'll be in those trunks,' he said as they came in. He pointed across the room. 'Let's take knapsacks, too.'

They grabbed the clothes as quickly as they could and ran back outside into the trees.

Even though the uniform didn't fit, Lexi was glad to get rid of the bulky dress and the basket. All she kept on of her Paris clothes were the shoes, since they fitted her well and looked enough like boots. She rolled her sailor's pants up at the ankles and pulled the belt in as far as it would go.

Doug jumped from Al's hand and into his new pack as soon as he caught a hint of sausage. It was empty. He pressed his face against an oily stinky sausage stain and dreamt of the real thing.

Will rolled up his Paris pants and folded the jacket. 'Might as well take these,' he said, pushing them to the bottom of his pack. 'We might need them again, and they'll make the knapsacks look full.'

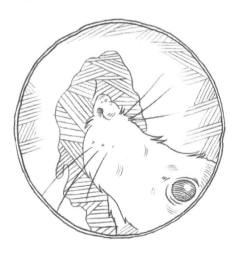

In his German uniform, Will could disappear easily into this war. Lexi watched him load his pack and wondered how much longer he would be with them. He could leave at any moment, change into his French clothes when he wanted to and somehow make his way back to London. Since they'd arrived in 1918 she'd been dreading the moment when Will would turn to her and awkwardly begin some goodbye that would leave her with Al in a foreign time and place, with a portal to find in a war.

Will noticed her watching him. 'Pretty convincing, don't you think?' He saluted her, in the style he knew the Germans used. He took his key badge from his pack and pinned it to his lapel. 'Better put yours on. Your grandad could be anywhere, maybe even in a tunnel near here.'

They found the path the two Germans had taken and followed it around the hill to a rough road running next to a train track. At the far end of the track was the Kaiser Wilhelm. It looked like a huge train carriage with a long pipe swung way up into the air from one end.

A sailor stepped out from behind it and waved a flag. There was a boom as the gun went off again and bangs as other guns went off as well. From the train track the word hunters could see them dug into the hillside.

'That's the noise we heard when it fired before,' Will said as he worked it out. 'Other guns. They're trying to mask the firing of the big gun. If they fire the others at the same time it'll all sound pretty normal at our frontlines. Then the shells from the others'll land there, so no one'll know another gun's gone off and there's a shell on its way to Paris.'

There were two armed sailors next to the track as the word hunters approached the Kaiser Wilhelm. They were deep in a conversation about where they would go on their next leave. One of them half looked over and nodded and the other didn't look at all. Al wondered if there had been guns back at the barracks. They'd be no help, though. The moment they needed guns, they would already have lost. There were more sailors around the carriage, most of them with weapons. And they knew how to use them. Al didn't. He could count ten sailors and there would surely be others out of sight.

The only thing for the word hunters to do was walk as if they belonged there and had no doubts at all.

As they reached the mouth of the tunnel an officer shouted, 'Ordnance!' It seemed to be to them.

'Yes, sir.' Will saluted as he said it and Lexi and Al followed.

The officer pointed off into the dark. There were lamps in the tunnel, but not many. Grandad Al would never see their key badges in there. The tunnel had been cut roughly into the rock and threw up shadows. It was easy to imagine a man hiding there, waiting. Grandad Al, waiting for the next word hunter to come to the portal. Not waiting for a detachment of three German seamen.

'What's ordnance?' Lexi said to Will, once they were away from the officer.

'That's the shells. He's sending us to the shells.' Will could see them on a rack against the wall.

Three men were standing there with a trolley. Two of them turned to the rack to lift the next shell.

'Hold on,' the other said. 'Here's our relief.' The two men immediately stepped away from the rack. 'Nice of you to turn up early.' He looked at the word hunters more closely as they approached. He couldn't see them well, with the tunnel mouth and daylight directly behind them. 'You're new, aren't you?'

'Yes,' Will said. 'First time. Just posted here. What do we need to know?'

'It's just like gunnery school, but with a few extra steps. The shells are numbered.' He pointed to the rack. Each shell had a number written on it in chalk. Twelve was next. 'They have to go in their exact order. It's not a normal gun. The shells go faster than any shells before. They wear the barrel away, but each one needs to be a perfect fit, so each shell is very slightly bigger than the one before it. Put a shell in too early and it might burst the barrel. The engineers'll decide when the barrel's had its time.'

He led them to some weighing scales that were near the trolley, and he handed Will a book and pen.

'Here's the other difference.' He opened the book to show the numbers 1 to 20, running down the page, with two

columns of figures filled in next to them as far as 11. 'You need to weigh and measure the length of each shell, record it here and report it to the gunnery officer. He needs that to get the barrel height right. It changes with every shot.' He looked past Will at Lexi and Al, trying to see them properly in the dark. 'We're taking them young now.' He shook his head. 'I suppose if I ask how old you are, you'll say 18. Well, you'll grow up fast here. This'll put muscles on you. These things are mostly steel. They take some lifting.'

'Enough lecturing, Heinz,' one of the other men called out. 'They're our relief. Let them relieve us. Then you can get back to the real work of telling us all about your girl in Metz.'

'I know I only met her once, but—' He shrugged. 'It was a great letter. You just wish you'd got a letter like that. You just wish *you* were going back to barracks to write to a girl like her.'

All the way out of the tunnel, Heinz was insisting it was the real thing and the others were saying that she'd have forgotten him already.

Al remembered the Anzac letters home that he and Lexi had studied at school. The Germans wrote letters, too. Of course they did.

Will went over to the shells and put his hand on number 12. He rubbed the chalk 2 and it blurred.

'Let's swap them.' He wiped his hand on the rack. 'Let's take them a bigger one next and see if we can blow the barrel.'

'But that's changing history,' Lexi said. 'We're here for the portal.'

'And we'll find the portal, but if we take this gun out we'll save some lives in Paris and our armies can focus on the spring offensive. The war will still be over in 1918, and probably no earlier, unfortunately. I know we're not supposed to, but I'd like to change this bit of history more, if I could. I've got a brother not far from here, and two cousins. Anyway, we have to go to the gun. It's the portal. That's how this one works.' Will could remember it from the other three steps. 'Let's give them 17.'

As he smudged the crossed German 7 with his hand, Lexi was sure he was about to leave. He'd take them right to the portal and she knew she should be grateful for that. He could have left them in Paris. They had got through battles without him before, but she wished 1918 hadn't come so quickly.

It took all three of them to lift the shell and they could only hold it for a few seconds before putting it down. It took them four goes to get it to the scales. Will didn't even look at the weight. He looked at the figures in the book for numbers 9, 10 and 11 and estimated what 12 would be. He did the same with the length, as Al measured the shell with a tape.

With one more lift the shell was in the trolley, and they pulled it forward across the uneven ground and out of the tunnel to the rear of the gun.

'Come on, come on!' one of the gunnery crew shouted, as he saw them coming. 'We should be loading already.'

He swung a small crane around and they lifted the shell into its steel basket. He winched it up to the height of the deck and the word hunters climbed the metal steps to help him unload.

There was a picture stencilled onto the base of the gun barrel. It was all white – the face of a man with a neat beard and moustache and a pointed helmet. Will noticed it and touched Lexi's arm. It was Kaiser Wilhelm.

They lugged the shell forward and loaded it. The gunnery crewman closed the barrel and locked it. Will presented the figures to the officer in charge, who recorded them in a book of his own and calculated the adjustments he would need to make.

'Number 12,' he said as he turned a wheel to make a small change to the barrel height. Cables reached up from the gun base to a structure rising from the barrel like the pylon of a suspension bridge. He stepped behind a steel barrier and turned a key in a control panel. 'Another gift for Paris from Kaiser Wilhelm.'

As soon as he said it, one of the Kaiser's eyes in the picture started to blink and then to glow.

Al slipped his pack off and found the activated peg. Together the word hunters moved forward.

'Will,' Lexi said. 'Step back. It's your chance. It's your year. Go now, while you can.'

The Kaiser's eye was within reach.

Will didn't move. 'I'm coming with you. Caractacus'll get me home. There's something going on with those men in grey robes. Something bad. It's up to us to deal with it. And I think you're about to bump into a few more of them.'

'Stop! Stop there!' the gunnery officer shouted. 'Get behind the shield. We're firing in ten seconds.'

Will stuck his thumb in the Kaiser's eye and it opened up. Al pushed the peg in, locked it and turned the key.

'Jump!' The gunnery officer shouted. 'Cover your ears and jump!'

Mist rolled along the train tracks and poured into the tunnel. The gun carriage shook and swayed. The signalman with the flag took a step away and vanished in the haze.

As the word hunters passed into the portal there was an ear-splitting wrenching explosion.

1648
—
Colchester
England

MACROPHOTOMATIC

HEY FELL AND the explosion was gone, like a sound effect turned off before it had finished.

They hit bumps and then clear cool air, first dropping quickly and then gliding down. As they broke cloud they saw a walled city below, with houses and farms around it. On one side it was under attack by an army of thousands of soldiers. There was a puff of smoke from the city wall as a cannon fired.

The army was retreating. Men were stumbling across fields and through hedges as the soldiers on the walls fired down on them.

The word hunters were falling towards a farm.

'Swerve!' Lexi called out, when she worked out the details of the farm below. 'Pig sty!'

She had landed in enough pig sties already. They steered clear and came down on dry ground beside the pigs, just as a chunk of smouldering twisted metal hit the mud in the sty with a splash and a hiss of steam.

'What?' Will jumped further away. 'That—' Then he worked it out. 'Kaiser Bill. That's why that didn't happen last time. It's a bit of the barrel. Looks like we stopped the shelling for a while, at least.'

Lexi took a look at what they were wearing. Their backpacks were now sacks and she had on a rough off-white dress with a cord around her waist for a belt. Al and Will had shirts with puffy sleeves, breeches and stockings that came to below their knees.

They weren't soldiers. The soldiers were streaming back into the farmyard from the city and they were wearing steel body armour fitted tightly over red jackets. They had round helmets with brims that came to a peak at the front and they were carrying long poles that ended in steel-capped points or blades.

'Pikemen,' Will said to Lexi and Al. 'Great for holding cavalry back, but no use at all for attacking a city wall. The city's Colchester. It's the Civil War. The English Civil War. 1640s. We're farmers.' He took his eyes off the soldiers for a second to glance at Lexi. He smirked. 'And a milkmaid.'

'Why is the past—' She took the bonnet from her head and scrunched it up. 'Why does it have to be so sexist? Why can't I be a farmer?'

The soldiers were regrouping in the farmyard. They had mud on their stockings and up their grey breeches. A couple had lost their helmets and another had lost his pike. One who seemed more senior was trying to convince the rest to rejoin the attack on the gates.

'But what about Humpty Dumpty?' one of the others said.

'Humpty Dumpty?' Lexi laughed. 'Humpty Dumpty sat on a wall?'

With that every soldier stopped talking. Lexi hadn't meant them to hear it. She had flown over World War I, dressed as a German sailor, blown up a gun, fallen 270 years and only just been able to focus enough to avoid a pig sty. She had escaped one war only to land in another without a second to think it through.

'Are you laughing at us, girl?' one of the soldiers said. He reached out and prodded her in the chest with his pike. 'What are you? Some kind of royalist?'

The word gave the other pikemen something to focus on.

'Royalists!' one of them called out, and they all swung their pikes forward. They pinned the word hunters against the farmhouse wall and suddenly they all had something to shout.

'Throw them in a ditch!'

'Throw them in the pig sty!'

'Stuff them in a cannon and shoot them into Colchester!'

'Don't worry,' Will said to Lexi. 'This one always goes like this.' From the city walls there was a boom, then a crash not far away and screaming. 'That's Humpty Dumpty. A big fat cannon up on the city walls shooting down at the brave parliamentary soldiers trying to break through the gates. But I think we know what they have to do.'

'Yes.' Lexi looked straight at the man whose pike blade was pointing at her neck. 'You need to make Humpty Dumpty fall down.'

'You need to bring down the wall under Humpty Dumpty.' Will wanted to make it as clear as possible. 'There's a weakness there.'

'Oh really?' The soldier in charge sounded as if he didn't believe it for a second. 'Really, farmhand? You're an expert in sieges, then?'

'I can help with this one.'

'Come on, George,' one of the others said to the commander. 'Nothing else is working. We're looking like fools and we're getting shot at.' There was a murmur of agreement, so he went on. 'The lord-general wants Colchester breached and we won't do it with pikestaffs.'

One by one the men lowered their pikes or lifted them back to their shoulders. They waited for Will to tell them more.

'You'll need your mortars,' he said. 'You'll have to train them all on one spot – the walls at St Mary's church, exactly below Humpty Dumpty.'

'Next you'll be telling me to have my cavalry ready to charge right after the wall's breached and follow that with infantry.' The commander was still not impressed. 'You realise I'm in charge of—' He did a quick head count. 'Twelve pikemen.'

'You know the attack is going nowhere, even if your generals don't,' Lexi said. 'This is your chance to change that. This will change the battle and you'll be the one suggesting it.'

That gave him something to think about. He had no desire to rush the gate with his pike again and the farmhands were right that it would get them nowhere. If they were also right about the wall, he might just end up the hero of the battle. For a moment he imagined how well it might work out. He would be sent home with a pension for life, perhaps granted a small manor house and land. Children would perhaps sing songs about him as the man who brought down Humpty Dumpty.

By the time he found his captain, he was quite convinced. He talked the captain around too and the captain took the plan to a more senior officer in charge of a mortar company, by which time George, the platoon commander, didn't seem to rate a mention.

The mortar officer took the idea – his own idea, as it now seemed to be – to a colonel, who thought he might be knighted for having come up with it if it worked. He took it to Sir Thomas Honywood, who was in charge of all the troops from Essex.

By the time Sir Thomas Honywood presented his cunning plan to Lord-General Fairfax, the lord-general was so impressed he immediately said, 'That's the best idea I've had all day.'

'Don't worry,' one of the pikemen said to George, who had long ago realised there would be no pension and no manor house, and that he wouldn't appear in the song. 'At least this way, if it all goes wrong, someone else'll get the blame and we can get back to throwing these three into a ditch.'

As the afternoon went on, the lord-general and his senior officers put together the details of the plan. The wounded and dead were brought in from the fields and the word hunters were fitted out with their armour.

A kitchen had been set up at the next farm, with huge pots of stewed vegetables and a table piled with bread. Doug scrambled to the top of Al's sack, but Al grabbed the neck of it before he could jump out. As he reached the front of the bread queue and grabbed a piece for Doug, Al noticed initials carved into the table – 'TH', 'VH'. Then, written in blue ballpoint, 'AH'. Grandad Al had been here.

'He got past Kaiser Bill,' Lexi said. She looked across the fields to the walls of Colchester. 'Maybe this is it.'

She didn't want to count the number of times she had thought that. Or hoped it.

There were soldiers all around them. She pulled her collar out from under her armour and straightened it to make her key badge visible.

As they gathered to eat with the pikemen, Lexi put her bowl down and took the photo of Grandad Al from her sack.

'Have you seen this man anywhere?' She held the photo out. 'He's one of us. From our village. He might have gone in during the earlier attack.'

The man passed the photo around. Each one shook his head.

'Can't even see the brushstrokes,' one of them said as he turned it over to check the other side. He ran his finger across the paper, then held it to his face and sniffed it.

'It's a new kind of printing,' Will told him, hoping that would be enough.

'Message from the captain,' a man said, breaking into the group. 'We move at nightfall.'

As the sun set and the sky darkened the pikemen moved forward past the mortar battery. Each of the word hunters had a heavy pike over one shoulder and a short sword at their belt. They had practised formations with the rest of the platoon – going down on one knee to defend and digging the base of the pike into the ground, then standing to attack with the pike shoulder high.

In the fading light the mortars looked like cement mixers, each mounted in a metal cradle on a solid wooden platform.

As they crossed the fields and took their positions they could see torches up on the battlements and sentries on each tower.

The mortars began the battle. They sounded like fireworks being launched, but deeper and louder. The mortar bombs passed over them, high in the air, and then crashed down around the wall. Some landed short, splattering mud everywhere. Some landed on the battlements, breaking chunks of stone away. The walls held.

More troops appeared on the towers. In the torchlight, the word hunters could see them lifting their muskets and shooting them off into the dark in the hope of hitting something. Humpty Dumpty fired with a boom, but the crash as its shot landed came from somewhere near the gates, on the open road.

The mortars fired again and then reloaded and fired a third time. The walls showed damage as the third round of bombs exploded, but they seemed to be holding. Then the fourth volley came and this time three bombs landed together at the base of the wall, directly below Humpty Dumpty. There was a boom and a shower of stone fragments. As the smoke cleared, a crack could be seen in the moonlight, reaching halfway up to the battlements.

Without any further attack the crack widened. Stones dropped to the ground. The wall started to buckle and sag and then the battlements and the great cannon tipped over and thumped down into the mud, dragging most of the wall with them.

Someone ahead shouted, 'Humpty Dumpty's down!'

Humpty Dumpty's DOWN!

There was a cheer from the parliamentary troops, who took it as a signal to charge. The front pikemen ran for the gap with the steel points of their pikes jutting out ahead of them. They reached the rubble and the infantry moved in beneath their poles and started hurling the fallen stones clear by hand, allowing them to keep stepping forward.

The word hunters were well back in the column, pikes tilted vertically. The man in front of her was so big Lexi could hardly see a thing. She rested the base of her pike on the ground and took a half-step forward whenever the others moved.

There was shouting ahead, and clattering. Muskets fired down from the battlements, but most of the time they missed. The parliamentary musketeers moved in behind the pikemen and returned fire. Lexi watched them reloading in the dark, driving ramrods down their gun muzzles, before sending more shots fizzing towards the top of the wall.

Someone nearby got hit. There was a groan and a body fell. She stuck close to the man in front. A bullet would have to pass through him to get to her.

'There it is!' Al was pointing past the pikeman in front of him and at the base of the wall.

As stones were shifted from the ruins of Humpty Dumpty, the golden pulse of light was plainly there on the barrel of the gun.

'Clear to charge!' someone shouted. 'Clear to charge!'

Al changed his grip on his pike, ready to lift it to his shoulder. He took a deep breath and braced himself to run to the gap in the wall.

But the other pikemen were scattering.

He could hear the hooves behind him, before he could see the cavalry: hundreds of horses charging in the dark across the fields. Mud flew as they surged past and the ground shook with the weight of the horses' bodies.

The forward pikemen and infantry moved clear and the cavalry hit the gap in the wall at a gallop. From inside Colchester voices could be heard shouting and screaming as the horses plunged into the royalist pikemen, who were scrambling into defensive formation.

'This is it,' Will said. 'We're going in and the grey robes are there. We'll be carried past the portal, but we'll double back. Stick together and go for your sword as soon as anyone gets past the pikes.'

Al felt his mouth go dry as he moved his hands on his pike shaft. By the time anyone got past the pikes they'd be a few metres away. He didn't know how he'd draw his sword in time.

Then there was no time to think and they were moving, pressing towards the gap and then through it, spreading out across the street and trying to hold formation as they pushed into the royalists, pikes clattering like oars. Musket shots cracked from above. Riderless horses ran wild, rearing and kicking. A house started to burn.

In the dark and the clamour, Al had no idea who was an enemy and who wasn't.

The man in front of Lexi took a pike in the chest. It punched the breath out of him and buckled his armour as it passed through. He dropped his own pike and fumbled for the shaft of the one that had struck him, but he had no fight left.

Will shouted, 'Move!' and flung his pike away.

Lexi and Al followed and they all drew their swords.

A royalist swung his pike at Will, who ducked and deflected it. Next he lunged at Al, who ducked the pike, but slipped on the cobblestones and fell.

Lexi brought her sword down on the pikeman's arm and felt the bones crunch through the sleeve of his jacket. He dropped the pike and staggered backwards.

Around them the battle reached new heights, as more royalist reinforcements arrived and more parliamentary troops made it through the breach in the wall.

'The gates! The gates!' a parliamentary captain shouted.

The lord-general had added that to the plan. If the city

gates could be opened, the army would have a second entry point. There were fresh cavalry heading there now.

'Watch out for grey robes,' Will shouted, as the troop movement carried them forward. 'This is where they nearly got me last time, a bit further down here.'

He stepped into a doorway and Lexi and Al followed. Soldiers pushed past and new battles broke out ahead. The fight carried into other streets that were further away. Stragglers at the rear jogged past with pikes on their shoulders or swords in their hands, heading for the battle at the gates.

Some parliamentary troops stayed behind, guarding the street corners and the breach in the wall in case retreat was necessary. A horse cantered across the cobbles shaking its head. A hoof connected with a fallen pike and the shaft rattled across the stones and rolled to a stop.

Just as it seemed all was calm, two men in grey robes slunk by. They looked like monks until the fires from burning buildings glinted on their swords. They were scanning the street methodically as they moved along it. The word hunters pushed back into the dark. The two men rolled the body of a soldier over and emptied the leather pouch he was carrying onto the ground. They chanted in Latin and one of them made the sign of the cross, while the other went through the contents of the pouch. He took nothing and then checked the front of the soldier's jacket.

'They're looking for us,' Lexi whispered as the men crossed to the other side of the street. 'Looking for word hunters. They checked him for key badges.'

As she said it the men knocked on a door opposite and it opened. The room inside was dimly lit, but there was enough light for the word hunters to make out the shape of someone in there, tied to a chair.

'That's got to be one of us,' Al said as the door closed. 'It's got to be a captured word hunter.'

'I didn't see that last time.' Will stared at the building, trying to remember it. 'I fought a couple of them off then got back to the portal. I never saw that door open. How do we do this?'

'Let's get them to do it.' Lexi pointed to a group of parliamentary soldiers guarding the street. 'Let's go.'

She led the way across the street and told the soldiers she had seen royalist cavalry officers trying to hide. They had lost their horses and put grey robes on over their uniforms.

'Officers, were they?' one of the men said. 'We could do worse than catch ourselves some officers. Can't leave all the glory to everyone else.'

She pointed out the door and the soldiers didn't even stop to talk it through. They ran over and kicked the door in. It splintered over the table that the men in grey had moved to block it and two pikemen shoved their pikes across the tabletop. One man inside fell back and the table tipped over. Its candle hit the floor and went out.

Someone swung a chair at the pikes and their points scraped against a wall. The soldiers moved in with swords and the men in grey came forward to meet them. The soldiers had the numbers and drove them back, forcing them most

of the way to the far corner, where a row of stubby candles burnt over a rough hearth.

The word hunters ran to the man who was tied to the chair. He was in his 40s. He wore a key badge on his coat.

'Grandad Al!' Lexi said. The shock made her forget the fight for a moment, and the danger. The light was dim and half his face was in shadow, but –

'I don't—' He saw Lexi's key badge glinting in the candlelight. He tried to stand, but the ropes caught him. 'I'm Alan Hunter. I'm one of you.'

'Yes, you're—'

There was a groan at the far end of the room. A soldier dropped back from the fight, holding his arm.

'You're one of us,' she said.

Will and Al used their swords to hack through the ropes holding him to the back of the chair. Lexi knelt on the floor and started sawing at the rope around his ankle. Something landed nearby with a furry thump, then there was a frantic scuffling and gnawing. Doug was at work on the other ankle.

Within seconds, cut and shredded rope was falling to the floor. They helped Grandad Al to his feet and he rubbed his wrists. Near the hearth a soldier's sword sliced through the grey fabric of a robe, but was deflected by steel beneath. The man in grey lunged and drove his sword into the soldier's stomach.

'Go! Go!' Will shouted, pushing Lexi and Grandad Al towards the doorway.

As they ran into the street, Grandad Al turned and shouted out, 'You know it's the gun? You know it's Humpty Dumpty?'

He picked up a fallen pike from the cobbles and ran with it in one hand. He looked fit, the way he had in the photos. Like a javelin thrower, like a man who could drive the pike through a door if he had to.

Lexi cried as she ran. She rubbed the tears away with her free hand and kept her sword ready. She felt Al's hand on her arm.

'We've done it,' he said. 'We've got him.'

They had found their grandfather and they were running with him away from a battle and through the streets of Colchester in 1648.

The sound of fighting was close again. Suddenly parliamentary soldiers spilt out of a nearby alley. There was the sound of hooves racing on cobbles and royalist cavalry appeared, charging into the men on foot.

The word hunters ran to the breach in the wall and scrambled across the stones outside. On the barrel of the broken gun the portal light blinked. Al went down on his knees and fumbled around in his bag until he found the peg. Will opened the portal and Al drove the peg in, locked it and turned the key.

As the first of the soldiers stumbled out in retreat, mist billowed through the gap in the wall, the fallen stones shook and the ground fell away.

$\mathcal{T}$HEY FELL CLEAR of Colchester in darkness. There was a bump, then turbulence and they dropped from the sky to a clear summer day.

Lexi and Al spun around in the sky until they saw him. Grandad Al was flying to their left in the posture they had all learnt from Caractacus. His hair blew back and he laughed as he plunged towards the ground. Their father laughed the same way.

There were fields and forests below, and an inlet where the sea came a long way into the land. They were falling towards the edge of it, to a town and a castle built on top of a craggy rock. There was a wide square tower at one end, a tall tower in the middle and there were turrets at the other corners.

'We want the tower that faces the sea,' Will called out, and tilted to glide to it.

The others followed, and they landed on the battlements in their best 16th-century clothes. Lexi wore a purple satin gown with pearls sewn into the diamond pattern on the front. The others wore black jackets with puffy sleeves that were slashed to reveal red fabric beneath. They had black breeches on, and silver-grey stockings.

'Now's your chance,' Will said to Lexi and Al. 'We've got time. And we'll be safe enough here.'

There was a group of people clustered further along the battlements at the top of the tower, with a ceremony underway. A huge cannon was mounted facing out to sea. Short and squat and made of solid iron with iron bands around it, in some ways it was the opposite of Kaiser Wilhelm. There were coloured ribbons decorating its carriage. This time there was no war.

'You saved me,' Grandad Al said, before Lexi or Al could speak. He rubbed his wrists again. 'I don't know how long I was in there.'

'Thirty years,' Lexi said. 'Or no time at all. Depends how you measure it. We're on the same word as you.'

He smiled. 'Yes, we have two kinds of time, don't we? We're the only ones who would understand that.'

'We're after you. The next word hunters.' Al wanted a better way to explain it. 'We got the dictionary from the library at school. Cubberla Creek. You're our grandfather.'

'But I—' Grandad Al blinked and put his hand up to block the sunlight. 'But Mike's 15. Julianne's 14.'

'Thirty years ago. Mike's our father. Lexi's and mine, in the 21st century. We found the dictionary in the wall of the school library. They're doing renovations.'

'Thirty years—' The thought of it was too much for a moment. He put his hand on the battlements to steady himself. Thirty years of one dark night in Colchester, tied to a chair with a battle going on. 'What have I missed? Noela—'

'Grandma Noela's okay.' Lexi wanted to help him through it. 'So's Dad. So's Auntie Jules. They missed you, obviously, but—'

'There's so much—' A tear ran down his face. He didn't seem to notice it. He stepped forward with his arms open and hugged them. He caught Will's eye. 'And you?'

Will smiled. 'No, just those two. Will Hunter, London, 1918. They picked me up in the 1830s. After losing me there – but that's another story.'

Looking past Grandad Al, he scanned the battlements again from one end to the other, checking for threats. Men in grey, any new enemy. It wasn't enough to know he'd been safe here last time.

'I was the one who hid the book there,' Grandad Al began. 'In the wall. Once I realised its power. You're so young to be doing this. How do you—' He hugged them tighter. 'I've missed so much. I want you to tell me everything about yourselves. And Mike. And Julianne and Noela.' The wail of bagpipes sounded from the tower. Grandad Al stood back and looked at Lexi and Al at arm's length. 'We can't be distracted. We need to get through this one and then we can talk. And then get back to Caractacus. We have to reach him. Luckily, plenty of words will take us there.' He patted his jacket where a shirt pocket would be and then noticed he was carrying nothing. 'My bag. It's still in Colchester. My pen—' He reached inside the jacket. 'I've still got my pegs, but they've got my bag. It's going to look very strange when the sun comes up the next morning in 1648. It's got my loudhailer from sports day.'

He felt dizzy again and crouched down and waited for the feeling to pass. His memory of Colchester was patchy. He had swept in with the pikemen. Then there was a fight in a doorway, then the room. Now he was free, 90 years earlier and with grandchildren he had never known.

'This one's Mons Meg,' Will was saying. 'Seven tons of cannon. No grey-robes here, last time I came through. No war either. We're celebrating the wedding of Queen Mary in France a few months ago. She's still there. She's been there since she was five. Her mother, Mary of Guise, is reigning in her absence. You'll see her up there. The gun came from France a hundred years ago for the Scottish to use against the English. But it's also good for weddings, parties, family reunions—'

He led the way along the battlements to a point where the walls turned towards the tower. Down below were hundreds of people from the town, waiting for the gun to fire.

'It all ends badly for young Queen Mary,' Will said over his shoulder. 'According to *Encyclopaedia Britannica*. And therefore the internet.' He glanced at Grandad Al. 'Did you have the internet in the 1980s?'

Grandad Al stopped and thought about it. 'The internet? No, not that I'm aware of. I know *Encyclopaedia Britannica* pretty well, though.'

They climbed the five steps to the tower roof and made their way to the back of the ceremony. A bishop was blessing the union of the absent queen and her French prince Francois. The audience were Scottish nobles seated on benches and a crowned woman in black on a high-backed wooden throne. There were guards all around, and priests too, but no one in grey robes.

The bishop finished with a prayer and stepped aside.

The sergeant-at-arms stood up from his stool next to the cannon and ordered the barrel greased. While two men worked on that, a third tipped a funnel of gunpowder into the firing mechanism.

The sergeant-at-arms lit a piece of waxed fabric and walked with it to the edge of the battlements.

'To Queen Mary and to Prince Francois!' he shouted to the crowd below. 'God bless their union and long may she reign!'

A cheer rose as he went to the cannon. He fixed the fuse in place and pulled the trigger. There was a fizzing sound as he covered his ears and then a boom. Flame and smoke roared from the cannon barrel and the cannon rocked back on its carriage.

The cannonball flew from the battlements and over the crowd and the town, towards the marshlands and the widening river.

Three long disorganised cheers came from the crowd below.

The queen put on a smile that didn't look altogether happy and, as she stood up from her throne, the nobles hurried to their feet. The bishop came to join her and together they led the procession of dignitaries from the tower.

As soon as she was out of view and while earls and countesses and priests were still at the top of the steps, the sergeant-at-arms leant back over the battlements and shouted down to the crowd, 'The shot's gone out somewhere over Wardie Mure. There's sixpence for the man who finds it and a penny each to the first six men there to help him bring it back to Mons Meg.' He went to pat the cannon, but the heat of the barrel made him take his hand away quickly. 'Those things cost money, you know, and we have only ten of them.'

Near the cannon's trigger the portal glowed brightly.

'Two more pegs.' Al had his hands in his black leather bag. 'One more step before we're home.'

Home with their grandfather, home with Will saved after they'd lost him in Nantucket. Al wanted to believe it was finished and that someone else could be a word hunter now.

The others stood back while Grandad Al touched the portal and it fizzed open. The peg slipped into the groove of the firing mechanism, which was still hot and smelt of burnt gunpowder. Al locked it in place.

'Hey, what are you doing?' the sergeant-at-arms called out, as Al turned the key.

A fog rolled in from the sea, over the town and the battlements, and before the gunnery crew could move, the word hunters were gone.

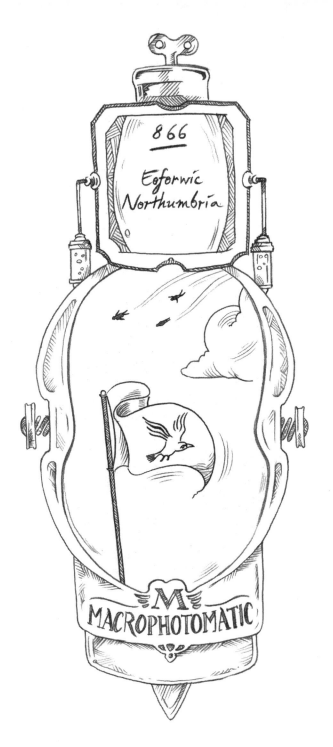

*T*HEY FELL AND plunged, then got thrown sideways. There was a clear drop that felt like centuries, then a shudder and another clear drop.

They burst from the cloud to a cold grey November day over forests, farmland and a river town. On one side of the town the farms outside the walls were already burning. An army was camped in the fields, all the way to the edge of the forest. There were tents set up in no particular order, and cooking fires and pens for horses.

The word hunters dropped to the ground near a tent made of bear skin. There were two banners flying above it, each one triangular with a curved lower edge and a design featuring a raven in flight.

'One guess what we are,' Will said, as he looked at the way they were dressed.

They all had leather helmets and body armour, and round shields. Will and Grandad Al had battleaxes, and Lexi and Al were carrying spears.

Grandad Al pointed to the banner over the tent. 'Two ravens. We're in an army fighting under the god Odin. He had two ravens. We're Vikings and we're about to sack some settlement.'

He slipped his hand under his chest armour and pulled

out a peg, just as Al did the same from the sack on his shoulder. They held them next to each other. The writing on them was identical.

'Eoforwic is York.' Will turned to face the town. 'We're about to capture York. The good news is we don't have to fight this morning's battle. I did that last time and what we're waiting for comes later on.'

The tent flap was thrown back and three men came out. They ignored the word hunters and one of them pointed to the town.

'That's where they'll come out,' he said. 'If we can bring them out.' He was pointing to a gate set into a wall made of heaped earth with wooden battlements on top. 'They'll make their battle formation there, so their archers can fire over them and we have to go up the hill to get to them.'

The tallest of the three men nodded. 'Are the berserkers at their breakfast?' He had an iron helmet in his hand and a bear skin over a tunic of chain mail. He carried it all as if it weighed nothing.

'Yes, my Lord.'

The tall man swapped the helmet from one hand to the other. 'I might say a few words to them.'

He led the way between two tents, heading for the far corner of the camp where men were starting to gather in an open part of the field.

'You're in the middle of the Great Heathen Army,' Will told the others as they started to follow the three Vikings. 'And that man – the boss – is Ivar the Boneless, Viking King

255

and son of Ragnar Lothbrok. Today's big problem for York is that its king, Aella, killed Ragnar last year by throwing him into a pit of snakes. Ivar's here for revenge. He landed in East Anglia, where they gave him hundreds of horses if he would leave in peace. It turns out that was exactly why he went there. He came here to attack York, and he wanted to surprise them by having cavalry. The best way for him to get horses was to turn up somewhere else and frighten them into handing them over.'

'*Encyclopaedia Britannica?*' Lexi could imagine him looking it up.

'Not this time.' Will leant the handle of his axe against his shoulder. 'Not for most of it, anyway. I got "Great Heathen Army" from it, but not much else. One of the berserkers told me the rest when I was here last time. I bumped into him when he was halfway through "breakfast" and he couldn't stop talking.'

'I've done "berserk",' Grandad Al said. He checked to see if the others had too, but they shook their heads. 'Walter Scott, then Old Norse. "Bear shirt" – that's a sort of translation of it. They wear animal pelts into battle. They're shock troops. And shocking troops too, as you'll see.'

Lexi caught Al's eye and smiled. It was the kind of game with words that their father would play. Shock troops that were also shocking. He held up a finger. They had a system for it. It was a Level 1 Dad Joke.

More soldiers were coming out of tents, strapping on armour, calling out to each other.

'Why is the king called Ivar the Boneless?' Ivar was still in front of them, and everything about the way he walked suggested to Al that he had the normal number of bones.

'He's very flexible. Apparently once he was attacked from behind and he somehow swung his axe back—' Will held his axe behind his head to show how difficult it was – 'and took the man's head off without turning round.'

'You'll be taking us home as soon as possible, right?' Lexi said.

'As soon as they say the magic word.' He brought the axe back down to his shoulder.

'It has to be the name of a gun, doesn't it?' She wanted it said now, whatever it was. She wanted to be home with her grandfather and to leave the Vikings and Northumbrians to fight whatever ugly old-fashioned battle they planned to. 'This one's been different. It's never been about the actual word, but they've all been guns with names. It's going to be a gun with a name and this has to be the name that gives us the word "gun".'

'But Vikings don't have guns, do they?' Al was pretty certain of it. 'And the people behind that fence don't either, surely.'

'Now I'm definitely not going to spoil the surprise.' Will looked like he was going to leave it at that.

Before they could push him any further, there was shouting from beyond the tents ahead of them – shouting and growling and thumping. They followed Ivar the Boneless past the last tent and what they saw made them stop suddenly and step back.

The noises were coming from hundreds of men in wolf skins, who were beating the shafts of their spears against their own bodies or smashing their heads into shields. One broke a stool over the back of another and they both waved their spears at the sky and roared like animals.

At a table an older man stood before a large pot with a ladle, pouring stew into bowls. The men in wolf skins were pushing forward to take it. Their eyes were red and they were shaking. Every muscle they had seemed to be tensed up and ready to fight.

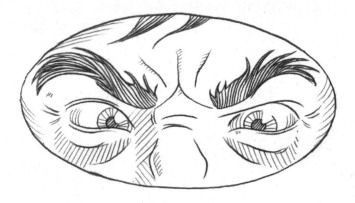

Mushrooms. Doug smelt mushrooms. Tasty, musty, spotty mushrooms.

He wriggled his way to the top of Al's sack and jumped free just as Ivar the Boneless stepped up onto the table and shouted, 'Berserkers!'

The men roared and turned to face him.

'Eat well!' Ivar thrust his sword into the air. 'Your next meal is blood!'

The berserkers bellowed and waved their spears. Sweat ran from their arms and their matted hair. One punched a shield until his fist bled and the shield broke with a crack.

'I'm so glad we're on their side,' Lexi said, taking a step behind Grandad Al without meaning to.

'This way,' Will said, 'or we'll get caught up in it.'

At that moment Al noticed a rat scurrying across the table towards the stew pot. A clean, well-fed 21st-century rat. Doug dodged around Ivar's feet and started scrabbling at the pot.

'Doug!' Al broke away from the others.

Lexi grabbed his arm to slow him down. 'We don't split up.'

As Ivar jumped from the table, Doug scrambled his way to the top of the pot. And fell in. The word hunters were only two steps behind Al when he got to the table. He grabbed a bowl.

The man with the ladle looked at him and shook his head. 'Not for you, Roger. You're not one of this lot. You'll live far longer if you stay away from this stuff.'

'Excuse me,' Grandad Al said. 'Those mushrooms—'

The man turned and Will stepped in and scooped Doug up in a bowl.

As more berserkers pushed forward, Grandad Al said, 'Some other time—' and moved back.

Al took the bowl from Will as they got out of the way. Doug looked up at him, fiercely bug-eyed with his lips peeled back and a low growl coming from his throat.

'How is he?' Lexi said.

Al couldn't take his eyes off him. 'Weird. Looks like he's doing backstroke. I think it's affected him. And why did that man call me Roger?'

Doug could see stars. Fireworks. And big pink – he didn't know what they were, but they were big and pink. And had trunks. And crazy, crazy eyes. And they didn't seem to like him at all.

He screeched and thrashed around. Al tipped out the stew and Doug slipped from the bowl and onto the ground. He ran around in tight circles. Ever-decreasing tight circles. He squealed something that sounded like 'Stella!' And then he vomited and fell asleep.

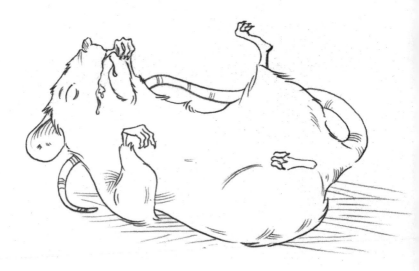

The word hunters sat on higher ground above the camp, next to the smouldering ruins of a farmhouse. Doug was still asleep, but his dreams had become a lot less twitchy.

'"Roger" was a joke,' Grandad Al said. 'Sort of. The man with the stew said "Hrothgar" but you heard "Roger", since that's what it becomes in English. You're a young guy with a spear. "Hrothgar" is an Old Norse or Germanic name meaning someone famous for his feats with a spear.'

Al wondered if his grandfather knew everything.

'I've got your history books,' he told him. 'I've read them all.'

'Really? I—' Grandad Al rubbed his eyes. He pictured 30 years, vanished. And this boy, whose life so far was less than half of that and who was more like him than he could put into words. 'That's great. I'm glad they didn't get thrown out.' It wasn't enough. Not nearly. 'I'm glad they ended up with you.' In the 21st century he would do better. When they were safe and his head was clear and the long Colchester night was not so recent. 'Has Caractacus asked you for a dictionary yet? I gave him a *Macquarie*. I told him it was like the Australian *Webster's*. He reads them, you know. Thoroughly, too. Is Macquarie still making dictionaries in the 21st century?'

'I'm pretty sure it is.' There was an old paper dictionary in one of the bookcases at home, but Lexi couldn't remember who had published it. 'Most dictionaries are online now.'

It wasn't an answer Grandad Al was ready for. 'On line? Which line?'

Will laughed. 'Just wait.'

In the distance from somewhere inside Eoforwic a horn blew. The gate in the town wall opened. Four men on horses rode out at the head of an army. They led the soldiers down the road a short distance and then signalled for them to spread out. Archers appeared on the wooden battlements. The soldiers lined up in rows, bringing their shields together at the front, with long spears pointing out ahead of them.

A horn sounded from somewhere in the camp and a cheer went up from the Viking archers, who were gathered on the slope facing the town. It sounded a second time and they all put arrows to their bows. On the third time they fired. The arrows went up and up and seemed to hang for a moment in the sky before falling on the Northumbrian troops, who had lifted their shields to meet them.

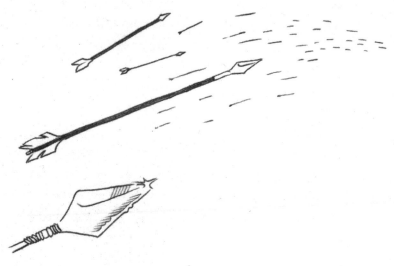

As the archers fired again, the berserkers charged. They ran through the ranks of regular Viking foot soldiers, shouting and screaming, like a pack of huge wild dogs. The archers kept firing as the berserkers hit the Northumbrian line, some running directly into spears, others smashing shields and stabbing anything that moved.

The Northumbrians' shield wall crumpled near one end, but the number of soldiers behind it held the berserkers back.

The Viking horn gave two short blasts and the foot soldiers moved forward. The archers lowered their bows. The Northumbrians closed ranks to meet the new assault. They were losing men, but holding their ground.

A shout came up from the far side of the Viking camp. Dozens of Vikings – perhaps a hundred – charged on horseback led by Ivar the Boneless waving his battleaxe with one hand. As his foot soldiers battled at the Northumbrian shield wall, Ivar and the cavalry struck the less protected flank of the defending army. Their horses trampled over soldiers and shields and Ivar leapt to the ground, swinging his axe as he landed. The others followed and the Northumbrian defences looked like collapsing.

The shield wall re-formed at the far end and the Northumbrian soldiers fought to get behind it. Ivar and his men kept coming. The Northumbrians backed away, closer to the town walls, and their archers sent arrow after arrow down on the Vikings. The attack slowed. The Vikings clustered together and brought their shields up.

The gates opened and the surviving Northumbrian troops scrambled inside as the Vikings dropped back.

They regrouped further down the slope, out of range of the archers.

The word hunters could see that Ivar was saying something, but they were too far away to hear it. He had two arrows stuck in his shield and he was thrusting his axe in the air, starting a chant among his army.

Once enough of them had picked it up, the sound carried. 'Gunnhildr! Gunnhildr! Gunnhildr!'

'And there it is,' Will said to the others. 'Gunnhildr. A woman's name made up of two Viking words for "war". They name all their big weapons after women, and this army has nothing bigger than Gunnhildr. She'll throw rocks that smash those walls. The name will stick. There'll be no record of her being here today – not anywhere, not written down – but in 500 years documents at Windsor Castle will say that there was once a great siege engine called Gunnhildr. The first gun. She's the portal. Let's go and find her.'

He led them into the trees, keeping them out of sight as they skirted around the Viking camp. Al tried to imagine what the very first gun would be like. He had Mons Meg in mind – a big fat cannon – but he knew it wouldn't be that. It would be a catapult, a trebuchet, a ballista. Something to fling rocks. He'd seen pictures, but all the names could get confusing.

The Viking chant kept going. 'Gunnhildr, Gunnhildr—' Stray horses were being rounded up and brought back to camp. Some men were returning with injuries. Will had seen

Gunnhildr come from the forest last time, pulled by a team of oxen.

Somewhere ahead through the trees they heard a hammer hitting iron. They crouched as they moved forward, making as little noise as possible. Suddenly Will's hand went up. The others stopped. He pointed through the trees. At the edge of the forest, crouched next to a line of bushes, were six men in grey robes. They were watching the Viking camp and the battleground, and waiting.

'That's where I came from last time,' Will whispered. 'I'm sure that's where everyone comes from, if it's their first time. It's where "TH" and "VH" put their initials.'

He didn't need to say what was going on. The men in grey were waiting to trap word hunters.

'Let's go to the portal.' Grandad Al's eyes stayed fixed on the men in grey as he said it. 'We need to get out of here if we're to do any good. There are six of them. They've got at least two axes and one sword. That's just what I can see. They probably have more.'

Will was about to disagree, but he stayed quiet. He signalled for them to go deeper into the woods. As they moved away Al looked around through the trees. He could imagine a man in grey robes behind every one of them, waiting with a sword and ready for word hunters.

'I think we should go back there,' Will said to Grandad Al once they were safely away. 'We could surprise them. Or persuade the Vikings to attack them. We could say they were people from the town trying to escape.'

'It's too risky.' Grandad Al looked back the way they had come, as if even talking about the men was dangerous.

'What about the next word hunter coming through?' Will wasn't letting it go. 'Those men are waiting.'

'There won't be a next word hunter while these two have the dictionary.'

'But what about what happened to me?' Will turned to Lexi and Al. 'We ended up in the same place at the same time, and I'm from almost a century before.'

'That's very rare.' Grandad Al kept his voice low and his eyes on the trees around them. Nothing moved or made a sound, other than the hammer – still beating out a rhythm – and the distant noises of the camp. 'I've just met my grandchildren. I'm not putting them at more risk than I need to. If the next hunter is with the Vikings right now, we may still have years to save them before they come this way. And we can do it, but not by charging in recklessly. We have to pick our battles, Will. You know that. You know how many battles there are.'

'But—' Will let the breath go. 'All right.'

He knew the other three weren't with him. And he could see the sense in what Grandad Al had said. If they charged the men in grey, surprise would only get them so far. Any one or all of them might be killed, perhaps for nothing. But he could also picture the next word hunter, searching for the portal, coming up the slope towards the trees.

They picked their path by the sound of the hammer, keeping wide of it until they were sure they were on the opposite side of it to the men in grey. As they got closer they could hear other tools at work. Through the trees they could make out two men planing a trunk that had just been cut down. Two others were working to fit an iron frame together. Not far away some twisted ropes were lying on the ground. At one end the ropes were loose, but at the other there was a handle, and from its centre came the blinking golden light of the portal.

Al reached into his sack for the home peg and his grandfather took his own from beneath his leather chest plate.

'You go first,' Grandad Al said. 'Leave your key in the peg. I'll pull your peg out just as the portal's closing and put mine in.'

'Aren't we going together?' Lexi put her hand over his peg. 'What if you get stuck here? We came all this way to find you. That's why we're doing this.'

'And you *have* found me.' Grandad Al checked the levers on his peg. They worked smoothly. He pulled the key in and out. 'I want to go back to my own time, to 1983. I want to be your grandfather when it comes to your time. If I go back with you now, I can't be. I'll be the same age as Mike and I won't be able to be me. I won't make sense. I want to be your grandfather. I have to take this chance.'

'He's right,' Will said. 'He's got a place in your century. And in your family. He should take it. We'll meet him there.'

He knew exactly why Grandad Al had to do it. Will had hit 1918 five years too old to go back to London. He could have made his way there and found the dictionary where he always kept it, but his 15-year-old self was still in London that March. Even if he'd waited until the day he'd got lost chasing 'hello', the 20-year-old Will couldn't simply step in and take his place.

Grandad Al had his own peg. Compared with the alternative, his plan would cost him 30 years. But Alan Hunter could have everything.

The men working on the siege engine started fixing the timber beams to the iron frame. When all four of them went to lift the final log into place, the word hunters moved.

Al hugged his grandfather as Will activated the portal, then Lexi hugged him too. She didn't want to let go in case it might be the last time. Second time and last. She wanted much more of her grandfather than that.

Will tapped him on the shoulder, reached out his hand and said, 'See you in the 21st century.'

Lexi locked the peg into place and turned the key.

As the wind rushed in and fog poured through the trees, she watched Grandad Al hold his hand up to wave. She told herself to remember everything – every feature he had, every word he had said in the time they'd been together – in case it was all they ever got.

As the portal flared and he lost them in the light, Alan Hunter stepped back a distance that he thought was exactly far enough to avoid being drawn in, and hoped that his guess was right.

Lexi, Al and Will flew through the trees and over Northumbria – away from the Viking centuries and the Normans and the wars with the French. Kings fell in battle and died in their sleep or of too much cider or lamprey, and new kings were crowned in their place. Cannons and muskets came to war, and then better cannons and better muskets. Engines turned the wheels of industry and sent ships into the wind. There were planes in the sky, then rockets and, back on earth, the great quiet work of medicines, the sound of music, the smell of rainforest and gum trees and a creek.

They landed in the park. Mursili was standing next to the dictionary as they dropped through the trees.

'You're all here,' he said. 'Good. I wasn't sure with it being "gun". I knew Will had done it before, but—'

'We found our grandfather,' Lexi told him.

Mursili looked around the park, then up into the treetops. 'Is he—'

'He's fine.' She felt dizzy. The ground beneath her seemed to shake and then steady again. She was home. And she'd met him.

She wanted him here, even if he was the wrong age. They would have found a way to make it work. But he was back with the Vikings outside York. Or somewhere else. Not here in the park.

'It's complicated.' As he said it, Will reached out to steady Lexi and she leant against him. 'He was captured in 1648. That's where he'd been all that time. Colchester. It was the men with the grey robes. They're after us. He had his pegs, though, so he was planning to make his own way home from the last portal.' He put his arm around Lexi's shoulders. 'Maybe it's worked. Maybe you'll see him and he'll get to be your grandfather. That's what he wants. And you know he couldn't do it if he'd come straight back with us.'

'What about you?' Al knew Will's position was different. He couldn't pull a peg out of a portal in the hope of getting his exact life back. His home peg had gone in the 1830s. 'I get why you didn't leave us in Paris, but—'

'I'll make it home someday.' Will looked across the park, towards their house. 'Caractacus'll get me back there when the job's done.' It sounded good. He hoped it was true. 'Anyway, people are expecting me at the hostel and the pizza's still cheap for another half-hour. Love this century.' He let his arm slip from Lexi's shoulder. 'I think you'll get to see him. He knows his stuff. Call me when he turns up, okay? We've got things to talk about once we've all slept this one off.' He noticed a bus coming along the road next to the park. 'I think that's got my name on it.'

Mursili turned around. 'Mine, too. All right. We'll get

together in a couple of days. I don't like the sound of those men who had your grandfather. You ran into them with "dollar", too. There's something going on.'

'And "water".' That was the first time and Al wasn't going to forget it. 'Just before we met you.'

Will jogged to the bus stop and Mursili took off after him. Lexi and Al watched them waving and the bus slowing down to pick them up.

Al picked up the dictionary and went to put it in his pack. Doug was asleep on his back, snoring, and Al lifted him up, shoved the dictionary in and rearranged his scrunched pair of gloves into a nest. Doug looked like he'd be sleeping for a while.

'I'm going to need that debrief with Will and Mursili,' Lexi said as they crossed the road to their house. 'Particularly if we don't—' She didn't want to think about not seeing Grandad Al again.

They were barely at the top of the front steps when their father opened the door. 'Where have you been?' he said. 'Your grandparents'll be here any minute and your junk's all over the lounge room.' He had his arms full of old newspapers and was on his way to the bin.

He ran straight past them and clattered down the steps.

Lexi reached for the handle of the screen door and then stopped. 'Did you know they were coming over?'

'Grandad Tom and Grandma Liz? No.' Al was sure he had checked the calendar on the fridge earlier in the day, and there had been nothing on it. 'I didn't even know they were in Brisbane.'

'Are they staying? I've dumped a lot of junk in the spare room.' She opened the door.

The TV room looked different. The TV was bigger and newer.

'Have you seen that vase before?' Al pointed to the bookcase at the end of the room. 'I thought we were only away for, like, seconds. Or no time at all.'

Their father rushed back in through the door. 'Talking or tidying?' He pushed past them to the kitchen and started loading the dishwasher. A car pulled up in the driveway. 'They're here. They're here already.'

Lexi found her phone between two cushions and shoved it into her bag. Al picked up a chip packet and stuffed it into his pocket. Two sets of feet started coming up the stairs.

'Knock knock,' Grandma Noela said, as she appeared at the front door. She had a sponge cake wrapped in a tea towel. She was dressed differently. She had running shoes on.

Behind her was a man with white hair and the beginnings of a stoop. He looked at them and smiled, as if nothing special was happening.

It was Grandad Al, 30 years older than he had been, seconds and centuries before.

Lexi burst into tears and almost dropped her bag. Al tried to say hello, but nothing came out.

'What's wrong?' Their father slammed the dishwasher door shut and ran out of the kitchen. 'What's going on?'

Neither of them could speak.

'Don't worry, Mike,' Grandad Al said, his voice as

strong as it had been in the 9th century. 'Lexi got her finger caught in a zip on her bag. Leave it to me.'

He put his arm around her shoulders and Al followed them out to the back deck.

'You and your bush remedies,' Mike said, but his father didn't seem to hear. He turned to his mother. 'Let me put that cake somewhere.'

'It's that time, isn't it?' Grandad Al said once he'd shut the sliding door behind them. 'You're just back from York, from "gun". You've just saved me.'

Lexi nodded and hugged him.

'I've waited years for this.' His voice shook. He cleared his throat. 'I knew it could be any month now. I knew you were old enough.'

'But how does this work?' Al said. 'Our whole lives are different now. If you hadn't disappeared—'

'I know.' He steered them towards the table and they all sat down. 'I've never been gone. Your grandma, your father, your aunt – they never had to go through that. That's what you two just did. Check your family photo albums and I'll be in them. But we know what really happened, the three of us. And you two know why my hair went white overnight after sports day in 1983.'

'But how do Al and I get to be word hunters?' Lexi looked into Grandad Al's face. It was more lined and the skin was less taut, but he was still the man from the photos she had looked at for years, still the man who had quietly turned himself into a warrior when he needed to.

'You found the book in the wall in the library?' He reached out and put his hand on Al's pack and smiled. He could feel the corner of it. 'When you saved me and I made it back home I kept going, but not long after that the dictionary went quiet. I kept checking for a few years, just in case. Sometimes I even took it home. Then I started hoping that might be it – that the words were all stable and the job was done.'

'Caractacus said that happens sometimes.' Al could remember it from their visit to Northwic.

'But it doesn't last, does it? Something's tipped it over again and it's found you.'

'Tea anyone?' Grandma Noela said loudly as she pulled the door open.

Lexi and Al could see their father looking out at them through the kitchen window. He pointed to his index finger and raised his eyebrows.

'It's okay,' Lexi called out. She rubbed her finger. 'Not as bad as I thought.'

Grandad Al said yes to tea and Grandma Noela went back inside as the kettle reached boiling.

'So, we can stop now?' Lexi wanted him to tell her it was over. 'We found you and you got home—'

Grandad Al's smile looked tired all of a sudden. 'If only. Someone has to keep doing the job. I'm sure Caractacus has been through all that with you. But things are far worse than he knows. It's not just a matter of making sure that language doesn't slip away.' He stopped and turned to check what was going on in the kitchen. Mike was slicing cake. Noela was jiggling tea bags. 'You know who Caractacus is, don't you? He's Merlin. You know the story of King Arthur? *That* Merlin.'

'Except that's a—' Al had read plenty about Merlin. 'Isn't it a mistake from the 12th century?'

'Yes, it is. I'm glad I gave you those books.' He could remember the moment. Al had been eight, nearly nine. It had been the first step towards getting him ready for what was to come. 'There was a Myrddin – a Welsh bard who, after one of the ugly battles with the Saxons, fled to the woods and became known for his visions and prophecies. That's where the name Merlin came from. At the same time our man was working with the British kings – Ambrosius, Uther Pendragon, Arthur – but it was a lost cause. It's from that work that the Merlin story began. To us he's called Caractacus, but even that's just a game he's playing. It's a name he's taken from a British king who lived centuries before. He almost told me that. He said, "You can call me Caractacus, if you like. There was one of them here once. They'll forget him soon enough, unless a few of us can keep him written down." He wants to stay invisible. He thinks we should all be invisible. He'd hate all that Merlin TV stuff being out there. We need to find him soon. We're going to need everything he's got to get us through what's ahead.'

'What do you mean?' Lexi didn't want anything to be ahead.

'Those men who took me, the men in grey who are turning up more and more often. We've been betrayed.

There's a hunter – I don't know when he's from, but he's raising an army and sending them across time. He's got some of Caractacus's powers. He's killing word hunters. He's killing the language. He's going to take power, long long ago, unless someone stops him. And who knows what he'll do if he gets it?' He heard footsteps inside. Noela was coming out of the kitchen with a tray loaded with plates of cake. 'Can you see what I'm saying?' he said quietly. 'If we don't stop him, the world – the English-speaking world at least – will be completely different. The language may not exist. The three of us may not exist. We need to get you ready to fight. With swords and bows, I mean. And to ride. The biggest battles we've ever seen are ahead of us.'

# WORD HUNTERS

## WAR OF THE WORD HUNTERS

# NICK EARLS &
# TERRY WHIDBORNE

It was late summer and Lexi and Al would soon be 13. They were survivors already, but not warriors yet. Will was the closest to that and, at 19, he was a good age for it too, even if he was technically 110. Which was nothing on Mursili, who had been born almost 3,200 years before and managed not to look a day over 35.

At least Mursili could handle a sword, even if it was in an ancient kind of way, and shoot a bow, and ride. He had been a Hittite boy before he'd become court librarian, and all those were part of a standard Hittite boyhood in the BC 1200s.

And now it was time to put the padding on and start fighting. Grandad Al lifted the gear out of the bag.

'I know it's hot,' he said. He had a motorbike helmet in each hand. 'We'll only do five minutes at a time. Who wants to go first?'

There was a pause and then Will said, 'Me. I'll give it a try.'

'And me.' Mursili swaggered across to Will and drew himself up to his full height, which put his head at the level of Will's chest. 'You probably don't need the helmet, but your femoral arteries are in grave danger, let me tell you.'

Lexi picked up a spare sword and imagined a shield on her other arm.

'What if one of them's coming at you from this way?' Al said to her. He was over to her right and he made a move in her direction. She lifted her sword to block his imaginary axe swing as she turned.

'Good.' Grandad Al clapped his hands together. 'You two work on the theory while these two get the gear on. And, Lexi, if Al's swinging something big at you, like an axe, just try to deflect it rather than take the full force of it with your sword. Your choice is right though. Use the sword if you can't get the shield there in time. And focus on the defence. You won't get to attack if you don't remember to defend. And remember, we're not there to win these battles. It's about staying alive.'

Al swung again and this time her shield arm was ready.

'So you're a Viking or a Saxon?' She couldn't really picture Al as either, but that wasn't the problem. She turned to her grandfather. 'What if he was a grey-robe with a sword? How do they fight? Are they like everyone else from whatever time it is or —'

She wanted the answer to be yes. She wanted Grandad Al to know, and something to be certain about the people who seemed to want to kill them.

Grandad Al looked at Will, who shook his head.

'I don't think we know,' he said. 'We don't know if they're gathering in some of the times we go to, or if they're being sent through time to find us. We might not be the only time travellers.' He couldn't help looking past her through the trees, checking. 'None of us has seen them after 1648. And they didn't take my pegs then.' It sounded like two pieces of good news, but it didn't amount to much. 'We have to assume the worst. They know who we are, they know what we do, they know most of what we know and if they've got swords we should expect them not to be surprised by the thrust.'

Lexi nodded, and tried to pretend that she hadn't wanted a different answer. Her friends from school were on their way to Madison Bond's house for a sleepover. They would play music, eat junk food, stay up late and take a thousand photos of the whole thing. Not a second of the evening would be spent discussing sword-fighting techniques. Sometimes it seemed to Lexi as if she had to be ready to ride into battle against the entire past, just to keep the present what it was – to make sure iTunes existed, and phones. As well as the English language and perhaps most of the people she knew.

She poked at the ground with the wooden sword. 'So, can I have the next fight?'

# ABOUT THE AUTHOR

NICK EARLS is the author of 16 books, including five novels with teenage central characters. *48 Shades of Brown* was a CBCA Book of the Year, and his other four young adult novels were Notable Books. *After January* was also shortlisted for the National Children's Literature Award, won a 3M Talking Book of the Year Award and was shortlisted in the Fairlight Talking Book Awards. The International Youth Library, Munich, included it in its White Ravens selection of international notable new books. It was the first of five of Nick Earls's novels to become plays. Two have also been adapted into feature films.

While the English origin of the name Earls is the old Saxon word 'eorl' or 'jarl', meaning 'village elder', in Nick's family's case it began somewhere totally different – in Arles in France. It's a place-based name. The family story behind it goes like this. When Hannibal of Carthage set out to attack Rome in 218BC, he established a base on the Rhone River before crossing the Alps. That base became a permanent settlement and took the Roman name Arelate, meaning 'town by the marshes'. Over time that name became Arles. (History records that some Greeks or Phoenicians were there before Hannibal, but the town was called Theline then.) Around 800 years ago, someone from Arles who had taken the place name as a family name moved to England. Over the years, various spellings emerged, 'Earls' among them.

# About the Illustrator

TERRY WHIDBORNE has worked in the advertising industry for many years, and is now recognised as one of Brisbane's most award-winning senior Art Directors. But as Terry's family grew, so did his interest in illustration. He began developing his style for clients such as *Vogue*, Virgin Blue and many of London's top ad agencies, before deciding that what he really wanted to do was concentrate on books, film and animation. Terry's first foray into books is the Word Hunters trilogy he co-created with Nick Earls. He lives in Brisbane with his wife and two kids.

To be honest, Terry didn't have a clue where his family name came from. But Nick, not for the first time, had a theory. Whidborne looked like a classic place name, but where was it? Nowhere. So Nick started factoring in spelling variations and thought 'Whid' and 'borne' had the look of old Anglo-Saxon (or possibly Celtic) words, though they weren't quite right. 'Hwit' – now written as 'Whit' – was though, and meant 'white'. After trying 'borne', 'born' and 'burn', he settled on 'bourne'. 'Whitbourne' meant 'white stream' and it turns out to be a town in Herefordshire in England. Then Terry found an old book confirming this as the origin of his family name.

# HAVE YOU READ
## *THE CURIOUS DICTIONARY*,
### THE FIRST BOOK IN THE
## WORD HUNTER SERIES?

### NICK EARLS &
### TERRY WHIDBORNE

Lexi and Al Hunter are twins with almost nothing in common – except their parents and their birthday! At school Lexi hangs with her friends, while Al hides in the library reading about history, battles and faraway places.

When the twins stumble upon an old dictionary, the world as they know it changes. They are blasted into history to hunt down words that threaten to vanish from our past and our present. Their lives and the future of the world are at stake. Can they find a way back home? Or will they be trapped in the past? For once, they'll need to depend on each other if they want to survive.

'An action-packed adventure story filled with humour, excitement and mysteries to solve.' *Kids Book Review*

'All-round fun and a little bit irreverent, Earls and Whidborne have created what is sure to be a favourite with a 9- to 13-year-old audience.' *Bookseller + Publisher*

ISBN 978 0 7022 4945 7